DO YOU REALLY NEED IT?

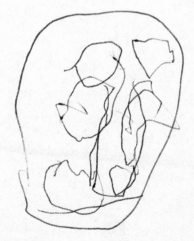

DO YOU REALLY NEED IT?

ONE QUESTION TO FREE YOU FINANCIALLY

PIERRE-YVES McSWEEN
Translated by Rhonda Mullins

Random House Canada

PUBLISHED BY RANDOM HOUSE CANADA

Copyright © 2018 Guy Saint-Jean Éditeur

www.penguinrandomhouse.ca

Random House Canada and colophon are registered trademarks.

Library and Archives Canada Cataloguing in Publication

McSween, Pierre-Yves
[En as-tu vraiment besoin? English]
Do you really need it? : one question to free you financially /
Pierre-Yves McSween ; Rhonda Mullins, translator.

Issued in print and electronic formats.
ISBN 978-0-7352-7365-8
eBook ISBN 978-0-7352-7366-5

1. Consumption (Economics). 2. Consumer behavior.
3. Finance, Personal. 4. Budgets, Personal. I. Mullins, Rhonda,
translator II. Title. III. Title: En as-tu vraiment besoin? English.

HC79.C6M3213 2018   339.4'7   C2018-902697-9
                                            C2018-902698-7

The translation of this work was made possible
with the help of a grant from SODEC.

SODEC
Québec

Text design by Terri Nimmo
Cover design by Lisa Jager
Interior images: (icons) © Picons.me; (silhouettes) © pablonis and
© glyph_studio, both depositphotos.com

Printed and bound in Canada

10 9 8 7 6 5 4 3 2 1

Penguin
Random House
RANDOM HOUSE CANADA

CONTENTS

FINANCIAL LEEWAY
DO YOU REALLY NEED IT?

You've never had a problem, and your life has been a long, tranquil river (is that possible?), but do you have $2,000 set aside, readily available? Do you have the money you need to deal with the unexpected? You know, that unexpected event that's just around the corner? (I'm talking about actual money, available in a few hours—not credit.)

In other words, do you have $2,000 ready to send to your daughter who went to Florida to live her dream, but who got in a fight with her boyfriend and wants to take the next flight home because she's scared?

Do you have $2,000 so your best friend can pay back his dealer . . . *this instant?* Can you help him in twenty-four hours? If you can't, either he isn't really your best friend or you don't have the money. You can always comfort yourself with the idea that, toothless or not, he's still a friend (and if the dealer is nice, he'll have spared him a few Chiclets).

I'm not actually suggesting you pay your friend's drug debts. What I *am* asking for is an honest answer to the question: "Do you have $2,000 readily available?"

And it's all relative; the amount will depend on your lifestyle, income, and short- and medium-term financial commitments. I'm just putting it out there.

The beginning of the debt spiral

Unforeseen events can trigger a debt spiral, whether we're talking about a sudden separation, a leaky roof, a business setback or a fluke accident only partially covered by insurance.

And yet these seemingly unpredictable situations are anything but. Statistically speaking, we know full well that the puck doesn't always bounce our way.

It's the law of probability: one day or another, the unexpected will strike. Then, like a friend in trouble calling you at 4 a.m., it forces you bolt upright in bed. Even before you have a chance to catch your breath, shots start coming from every direction, and you find yourself backed into a corner.

You need a safety cushion to deal with the unexpected. When you don't have a safety cushion, something as simple as a $2,000 balance on a credit card can turn into a ball and chain you drag around for years—at 19.99 percent interest.

People often point out that you can transfer that debt to your line of credit—which is true if your line of credit isn't already maxed out and the credit is available. But even if you use your line of credit as a cushion, don't forget that there is often a second and third costly surprise on the heels of the first. In fact, life is a long series of such surprises. So . . . do you have $2,000?

The stories behind the faces

People often tell me about their financial problems. The other day, a young woman told me that her credit card was maxed out, and she couldn't make the minimum payments anymore. She is thirty-five years old, with no savings and such overwhelming debt that I don't know when things will improve for her. Her distress was palpable. But her story isn't unusual, and that's sad.

Eventually, debt keeps you up at night. People are ashamed of financial failure. They don't want to ask for help, the way someone who is depressed doesn't want to make an appointment with a psychologist. Financial distress prevents us from seeing clearly or analyzing the situation calmly. And it all starts with an unforeseen event or a bit of bad luck that degenerates. It's not easy to explain to people that their past life has a lasting effect on their future life. **Without a significant increase in income, poor choices or bad luck can seriously compromise your future.**

In the face of financial difficulty, we tend to wait. To forget about it. We live in denial. Until the last payment cheque bounces. Often, at that point, it's too late. It's like waiting until you are a hundred pounds overweight before looking at your diet. But if you have the safety cushion of an emergency fund, you can start to turn things around.

You see people stretched to the limit every day. Financial precariousness has nothing to do with income; it's simply a question of a balanced budget and financial obligations. There are all kinds of professionals who earn extremely impressive salaries and yet are still short on cash. An emergency fund isn't a question of income. It's a question of foresight.

The availability of the emergency fund

The idea of an emergency fund is that you never want to use it. Like the fire axe behind the glass, it should only be used as a last resort. And the fund should be replenished as soon as possible afterwards.

As I note later (see "Saving: Do You Really Need To?," on page 108), a tax-free savings account (TFSA) is a good place for your emergency fund. It is less accessible than an ordinary bank account, and it lets you park income sheltered from taxes.

You need to protect your emergency fund from yourself and your desires. Desire is a bottomless pit: as soon as one desire is fulfilled, another is created. And to satisfy our desires, we are prepared to leap on our savings like misery on the poor. Desire isn't rational. It borrows from retirement savings and the grocery budget and drives us to buy things that have no immediate importance. Desire has a way of draining the blood from our brain and clouding our thinking. We shift from rational to impulsive.

Protecting your safety cushion means having a shield in the face of the unexpected.

How long would it take you to save $1,000?

It's a good exercise to ask yourself how long it would take you to save $1,000, and to keep that in mind the next time you feel like splashing out on something. For plenty of people it would take months. How do you deal with the unexpected if you can't pull together even $1,000 quickly?

Beyond after-tax income, there should be income available for desires—in other words, funds that are available once your financial obligations have been met. After your recurring expenses are paid for (housing, insurance, telecommunications, income tax, property taxes, clothes, groceries, savings), how much money is left over to treat yourself?

This exercise is also useful when considering any major expenditure. So, if you incur, say, $10,000 in consumer debt, how many years do you think it would take to repay that?

It's crazy when you see how quickly people can get their hands on $1,000 to satisfy a desire, and yet can't seem to save for a safety cushion. Obviously, planning for the unforeseen is a little dull. You don't invite your neighbour over to check out your flashy new safety cushion. No, the safety cushion doesn't turn heads. No one around you will notice it or admire you for having acquired one. But it alone can give you the confidence you need to face life without fear of jeopardizing your financial security or, worse, that of your loved ones.

Living without financial leeway

Not having financial leeway means being precariously perched on the branch of credit. You end up with a sore security ass. And that's uncomfortable. You can live with discomfort for a while, but you wouldn't want it to last.

After some time, the blood flow to your legs gets cut off, so that when an interesting opportunity arises, your legs are numb and you miss a chance to improve your situation.

A CREDIT CARD
DO YOU REALLY NEED IT?

Have you ever read the instruction manual for an iron? Being the kind of person who reads such things, I consulted the one that came with the iron I bought (yes, I really needed it). Among other salient points, the new owner was encouraged "not to place face against the hot iron."

I found the manufacturer's earnest warning amusing. They probably had to write it because one day some idiot stuck his face to an iron like a child sticking his or her tongue to a metal pole in winter—to see what would happen.

Risks aside, an iron is a great tool. And so is a credit card.

So, is credit dangerous? Yes, in the same way that an iron or a hammer is. Wielded properly, a hammer, like credit, is a powerful tool. I have a hammer in my garage. It can help me to build things, or it can be used for a murder worthy of *American Psycho*.

"Free" financing

Who has actually read their credit card agreement? Even after signing it? Very few of us. Credit card salespeople have us fill out reams of documents, at lightning speed, without reading them. How can you use your credit card properly if you don't know how it works? It defies logic, and yet that's what we all do.

Credit cards generally have the advantage of offering a grace period of at least twenty-one days. So when you get your statement, you have free financing for a minimum of twenty-one days from the statement date (from the date of purchase to the billing date). **Free financing is great, but how is that possible? It's thanks to people who don't pay on time.** There are so many of them that they more than make up for the people who do pay promptly.

Credit cards also offer rewards, which many find appealing. But the entire system is self-financing, at a profit. To take advantage of rewards, we implicitly contribute to the system in a number of ways. Here's how:

Every transaction gives rise to a charge to the merchant, calculated as a percentage of the total bill. It's a strange principle, given that a transaction, whether $50 or $2,000, takes the same amount of time to process.

Visa, Mastercard and other credit card companies make their money with these transaction fees. When you don't pay your balance on time, the bank that issues the card gets the interest. So the company that issues the card takes no credit risk with the client; it's the financial institution that owns the bad debt. Is that a problem? Not really.

When the bank's cost of financing is significantly lower than the interest rate on cards, it can stand to lose a few dollars to bad debt, provided others pay interest compounded daily at a minimum annual rate of 19.99 percent.

Perhaps people should start asking for a discount for anything paid for with cash. For example, someone buys a $2,000 bike. (Do they really need it? I will take a look at this issue in "High-end Equipment: Do You Really Need It?" on page 55). If a customer pays with a credit card, the merchant pays a fee. So it's in the merchant's interest to grant customers a discount if they pay with a debit card. If the method of payment doesn't influence the purchase price, then somewhere, someone is benefiting.

Handle cash advances with kid gloves

Short on cash this month? No problem. Just withdraw it from the bank machine using your credit card. Wait, not so fast. That's a cash advance.

Cash advances carry a higher interest rate than purchases. Why? Technically, when you withdraw money on a credit card, it's a signal that you need last-resort liquidity. Cash advances do not have a grace period. As soon as the money is withdrawn, it starts generating daily interest.

Cash advances are the worst thing you can do with a credit card. Would you pay over 20 percent in annual interest on a personal or car loan? Not on your life! But that's just what many people do with their unpaid credit card balance.

The interest rates on credit cards are high, which is explained by the nature of the product. Virtually anyone can have access to this type of credit without providing a personal guarantee. There are few barriers to entry—even with a bad credit rating, you can still get a credit card—and the interest rate reflects that.

Setting a much lower rate on credit cards would create problems for access to credit: less affluent people would no longer enjoy the benefits. So to create an equitable product, we have to pay high interest rates. And why would we want lower rates anyway? If people pay off their balance every month, the posted rate is irrelevant to them.

So why have a credit card? For the benefits.

Lower bank account fees: No more banking plans! When you pay with a credit card, there is only one monthly transaction in your bank account for day-to-day purchases.

Credit with no collateral

Free financing for at least twenty-one days: During the twenty-one-day grace period between the date the statement is issued and the payment date, no interest is charged.

Build a good credit rating: Making credit card payments on time and having a reasonable balance are two things credit rating agencies like Equifax look at. These things help you build a good credit rating (see "A Good Credit Score: Do You Really Need It?," on page 117).

Extended warranties on goods and services: Some credit card companies double or extend the manufacturer's warranty when goods are paid for by credit card.

Purchase insurance: Purchases made by credit card are sometimes insured against theft and damage.

Discounts on certain products: Sometimes you can get a discount of the "apply for a credit card and get 10 percent off your purchases" variety.

A method of payment that's widely accepted: These days, you can usually pay by credit card, except in stores that don't want to pay the transaction fees and those that don't want to declare their income.

A way to track your spending: Your statement gives you a description of every expenditure you make. With some cards, you even get an annual statement with spending sorted by category.

A record of purchase dates: If you keep your credit card statements, you can easily find the purchase date for an item and check whether the warranty has expired.

Rewards: Every time you use a credit card, you accumulate points toward the purchase of goods or services (if you use a credit card solely for this purpose, remember that the return is very low).

Make purchases online or by phone

Fraud protection: If you notify your bank that transactions have occurred without your knowledge, generally you don't have to pay for them.

Reduced risk of loss or theft of cash: I once had $200 in cash stolen from my wallet, and that money was gone forever. But if a credit card is stolen, you just report it and the creditor covers any purchases made on it.

Unnecessary insurance?

Life insurance on a credit card isn't very expensive. So why not take it? First you need to ask yourself whether, when you die, your loved ones will be saddled with debt. If they will, why would they accept the inheritance? If you leave an inheritance, will it be enough to pay off your credit card balance?

So why take the life insurance? To get the best return on your death? How do you know that, when you die, your credit card balance will be as much as the premiums paid on the life insurance?

I always decline life insurance on credit cards. It's a personal choice. You need to ask yourself whether you really need it. What is the risk of not taking it?

Don't forget that advisers at banks have to reach their sales targets for credit cards and credit card balance life insurance. You wouldn't ask a car salesperson about your needs, so why would you ask a credit card salesperson?

What should you buy with the points?

What is the best way to use credit card points? Save. Invest. Financial institutions sometimes offer RRSP investments in exchange for points. Instead of buying stuff you don't really need or getting gift certificates from a store, why not invest?

Financial institutions sometimes top up the investment when you accumulate a certain number of points. You could take advantage of a promotion such as "Get a $500 investment with 50,000 points rather than 55,000." But when it comes to investments, choose an RRSP or TFSA if they are available, because they are probably the only points-based products that won't make you consume more.

One, two or ten cards?

Is it really that bad to have several cards? Why not ask yourself the opposite question: why do you need more than one card? Hey everyone, look at me: I have six credit cards! Do you have six hammers, six irons or six lawn mowers? Credit cards are a tool. What is the point of having more plastic in your wallet?

Do you want a second card to whip out when the first one doesn't work for whatever reason? Fine. But in that case, the second card, which you would use sparingly, should have a much lower limit than the first. For example, if you have a credit limit of $10,000 on the first, the second should have a limit of $2,000.

Do you have cards just to get discounts in stores? What is the impact on your credit rating of having so many cards? It could compromise it (see "A Good Credit Score: Do You Really Need It?," on page 117). Simply put, every credit card is a new application for credit. It could be interpreted as a need for more credit and, as a result, a greater chance of inability to make payments down the road.

And if you miss a payment on a department store card, the interest rates are the highest of any credit card. If you aren't in the habit of making your payments on time, the cost of financing could be higher than the discount you get for using the card.

In short, do you want to trade a short-term benefit for long-term consequences? Around six out of ten Canadians pay the balance on their credit card on time. Why keep increasing the limit? How many times has a limit actually stopped you from buying something?

Credit is a tool that should be taken seriously; it's not like taking yet another slice of pizza after you've had your share. Credit card agreements are legal documents that confer rights and obligations. Credit cards are not renewable credit you are automatically entitled to—you have to show your ability to repay the balance in the very short term.

A method of payment, not financing

Credit cards are practical tools in a world where paying with cash is done less and less. So if you think of a credit card as a method of payment, that makes sense. **But once you fall into the trap of thinking of it as a method of financing, you put the noose around your neck.**

Before you buy something, you should ask yourself: would I be able to pay cash for this right now? If the answer is no, chances are it's beyond your means. And buying something on credit without having a repayment plan is like putting a forty-ounce bottle of vodka in front of an alcoholic. If you don't have the cash to pay for something, it's likely that will continue to be the case unless you start bringing in more money.

Buying is an act of impulse. For your brain, there is no difference between swiping your card through the machine to pay for something that costs $100 or $2,000. It's an automatic gesture. Only later do you understand the harsh, cumulative impact of your decisions. And that's a shame.

You really need only one credit card. What should you do with the others? Go to the drawer and take out another dangerous tool called *scissors*.

The end of this chapter could be an opportunity to hone your cutting skills. There might be an Edward Scissorhands of credit hiding inside you.

THE LATEST TECHNOLOGY
DO YOU REALLY NEED IT?

I remember buying my first LCD TV around 2013. Up to then, I made do with a cathode-ray screen.

People who came over were surprised to see, in the corner of the living room, the convex screen, a prolific producer of static electricity. But when broadcasters changed from the 4:3 format to 16:9, I had to rethink my long-term relationship with the magnificent 27-inch Sharp: the two black bands, which shrunk the image, made it so we had to glue our noses to the screen to see anything. It was annoying, because the television itself was still as good as new.

I had paid a little over $350, tax included, for it at the turn of the century, so it had an average cost of ownership of less than $30 per year. Its replacement was a flat-screen TV that cost $1,000. Despite my good intentions, the system finally got me: it made my television obsolete before it died a natural death.

The folly of the early adopter
What does being an early adopter of technology actually get you? Practically nothing. Okay, I will grant you

that in the 1980s, being the first to own a yellow auto-reverse Walkman impressed people for a few days. But owning the latest technology doesn't arouse admiration; it arouses desire. **The desire to enjoy a benefit that isn't really a need.**

Marketing plays a part in this. Who hasn't been in a store and got excited at the prospect of buying something? That excitement tends to ebb a few hours or a few days later, leaving regret in its wake. There is a feeling of emptiness after you buy something. If your life is empty, no matter what you buy, it will still be empty when you get home, even if you've arrived with your hands full.

Owning something doesn't add meaning to life, but experiences do. So **when you own something, you need to maximize its utility and ask yourself what benefit or joy you will get out of every dollar paid.**

If buying a piece of the latest technology at twice the price doesn't double our joy or satisfaction, save time, or deliver significantly more comfort, why do we buy it? Because deep down we have a false sense that the product will make us better.

Just think of the headsets people had permanently lodged in their ears a few years ago. You would see people at restaurants proudly wearing them, as if to say, "Over here! I'm just like Robocop!" Ridiculous.

The high price of technology

Manufacturers have to spend a lot of money on R & D to develop new technology. And then what do they do when they put a highly differentiated product on the market? They try to make the early adopters pay for the cost of technology development. To cover their financial risk, they bank on the excitement and frenzied consumption of the first group of people who buy their product. They want to profit from what is called consumer surplus: the willingness of one consumer to pay more than another.

The price strategy they use is called "skimming." The first buyers pay the big bucks until the price of the product drops, either because a critical mass of buyers has been reached (allowing for economies of scale) or because someone has launched a product that gives the original a run for its money.

Generally speaking, you should never buy new technology. Just think of the price of VHS recorders in the 1980s, the price of DVD players in the 1990s and the price of Blu-ray players when they first hit the market. A Blu-ray player originally cost as much as $1,000; today, you can get them ten to twenty times cheaper.

And just think of the fools willing to spend the night outside in order to get the latest Apple product before everyone else. What is Apple actually selling? They're selling the "privilege" to be the first consumer to own and use a technology.

The first consumers pay for those who follow, basically subsidizing them. So I want to say thank you to the people who line up at midnight to buy the latest version of a gizmo, because you allow me to buy the same product later at a fraction of the price. Next time, why not send a donation to the middle class and wait a few months before buying?

You can't even justify your early purchase by saying it will last a long time. According to the title of a novel by French author Frédéric Beigbeder, "love lasts three years"—and technology has a similar shelf life.

Obviously, you can use something for three years and then

commit to a longer-term relationship of five or six years, stretching out its use. But at a certain point, advertisers and your social circle will make you feel like a dinosaur.

In fact, everything is planned, even your desire to change. **People are puppets when it comes to spending.** We think we are making a thoughtful purchase, but the logic behind our purchase is often flawed. It doesn't make sense to buy new technology when you can repair what you have, buy used or just do without.

Planned obsolescence

With every advance in technology, planned obsolescence is at work. And technology is increasingly hard to maintain or repair affordably.

There are two main types of planned obsolescence:

1. The product stops working.
2. The product's utility is limited or out of step with the times given the scheduled release of a series of product enhancements. Just think of computers. Almost as soon as you buy one, a new one hits the market that is more attractive, faster, more practical and lighter.

You spend, therefore you follow.

The case of the washing machine

My mother kept her washing machine for nearly twenty-eight years. It was so old that the marks on the dial to indicate the cycle had worn off; she just knew to turn the control panel dial halfway.

The washing machine's mechanics made it simple and cost-efficient to repair. But things have changed over the decades.

Manufacturers have added electronic control panels with twenty-eight cycles and virtually the same number of options for each one.

I have probably used at the most three wash cycles in my thirty-eight years on this earth. But when I buy something, I still want the bells and whistles I will never use. The control panel is beautifully designed, but when something breaks, you can pay as much as the machine's amortized value just in parts and the repair person's travel. So you tell yourself that for $100 more, you could have a new washing machine, and before you know it, the old one is out on the sidewalk and a delivery truck is on its way.

You have come to the control panel of planned obsolescence.

You have pressed the button on the buy-something-new cycle.

Your consumer judgment has been hung out to dry.

The case of my brother-in-law and his phone

You have to know how to skip technology cycles. For instance, my brother-in-law went straight from a green-screen flip phone with a retractable antenna to a smartphone.

For years, he was offered intermediary technologies that were of limited use. What did he care about a colour screen? By skipping technology cycles, you finance the purchase you make when your old gadget is truly obsolete or broken.

Having all the latest technology is a recipe for financial disaster. **The desire to spend is endless; but your wallet isn't bottomless.**

The case of the automatic faucet

One of the latest needlessly expensive technologies is a faucet that turns on when something comes into contact with it. After decades of manual faucets, I gave in on this new model, which has perfected the art of enticing people to pour money down the drain.

And it was more frustrating than anything else. Yet before I bought it, I must have asked myself the question "Do I really need it?" three times. Now I owned an expensive tap that turned on when the spirit moved it. Instead of saving water, I was just swearing more. I finally solved the problem by taking out the batteries.

The modern slave

People who always buy the latest model to replace things are slaves to a system of renewable, planned consumption.

The example of cellphones is worth its weight in gold. For a long time people traded in cellphones for the most recent model because it was "free." But nothing is free. You have to be pretty naive at age forty to still believe in Santa Claus. Everything is built into the price; if your phone is free, then you're paying more for your package. As the French chemist Antoine Lavoisier used to say, "Nothing is lost, nothing is created, everything is transformed."

I'm not saying you should pass on all technology. I'm just saying be patient. Patient like when you stand in line at an amusement park for two hours for a thrill that lasts five minutes. Why not live your life during those two hours?

If it ain't broke, don't fix it. Why get new technology when the old is still good? The real questions you need to ask are:

- Why do you want to buy the thing?
- What void are you hoping to fill?

So, do you really need the latest technology? If your answer is "I want to live the good life" or "It's important to treat myself," maybe you're working too hard for no reason.

Work less, live more. If you stick to this principle, you'll be fine for a long time. And I don't just mean three years.

BRANDS
DO YOU REALLY NEED THEM?

When I think of Nike, I think of Michael Jordan flying toward the basket or Andre Agassi scandalizing Wimbledon with his colourful fashion statements (not to mention his wig). Over time, brands create strong images in our minds, and few of us are immune.

Having been exposed to brands our whole lives, we rationalize them and attribute value to them. It's like water torture and Stockholm syndrome rolled into one: after a brand hammers away at you every day, you end up liking it and then adopting it, even if it puts a serious dent in your budget.

Brands are powerful; it's as though we think wearing luxury brands will make us better people (high-end products also create this false impression). This is the result of conditioning. Purses are the perfect example.

What are purses for? Purses are used to carry personal effects and, incidentally, they are a fashion accessory. For some women (and men), they contain a few essentials, like ID, credit cards and keys. For others, they enable them to deal with any eventuality, holding everything from souvenirs from Expo 67 to perfume samples for a quick spritz.

Every object has its place in the purse, regardless of its size. Technically, the purse's primary purpose is to carry a wallet and keys, so it's ironic to see someone with a $1,000 designer bag who has been in the red on their credit card for months. **Big bag, shallow pockets.**

It's going to last me a long time!

You often hear the argument that something will last a long time. Luxury goods may last a long time, but so do regular products. Price may be a sign of quality, but rarely proportionally. Take the example of a $1,000 purse that will "last a long time" compared with a $50 one that won't last quite as long.

Let's calculate the ratio: $1,000/$50 = 20 (the ratio varies depending on the value of a regular purse). In this case, the designer bag has to last at least twenty times longer than the $50 bag to bear out the argument that it will last a long time.

So, if the $50 bag lasts two years, the $1,000 one will have to last at least forty years to justify the price difference based on durability. That's impossible. Even if the $1,000 bag actually lasted forty years, the owner would get tired of it long before then.

This is in addition to the fact that the buyer had to shell out twenty times more to buy it. So, economically speaking, buying a brand at $1,000 based on the idea of durability is nonsense.

In her handbag past, my spouse had two purses that stand out: a fake Louis Vuitton and a real one, given to her by a friend who got an employee discount on it. She went through the real one as quickly as she went through the $50 fake.

So why the price difference? Because ridiculous costs are built into the $1,000 Louis Vuitton. At most, materials and labour to make the bag total about $100. Everything else is down to shipping, advertising, marketing, distribution and so on.

Louis Vuitton having a flagship store on Paris's Champs-Élysées doesn't give the bag any more material value. Having a street presence merely increases costs, prestige and the gross profit margin of the value chain.

The price also means that the brand can have Jennifer Lopez and Xavier Dolan as spokespeople. **By glorifying the brand, they create desire and envy, and they build a personality. They are selling a dream, not reality.**

It's all well and good to wear a $2,000 Caroline Néron or Tiffany diamond necklace, but are they strictly more useful than a cubic zirconia necklace from the local jewellery store? Of course not. It's just that luxury has to be available to everyone, and everyone has to have access to a brand image.

For every budget there is a level of luxury in line with certain brands. For example, if you make $40,000 a year, a $500 necklace is a luxury. Millionaires also need luxury relative to their wealth, which is why abominations like $25,000 necklaces exist.

The value of brands

So why buy brands? Why be a walking billboard? Because we have been convinced that when we do, we are part of something bigger. But it's an illusory sense of belonging with no value. When we wear brands, we are probably admiring ourselves more than others are admiring us.

It's hard to deny that it's strange to be proud of wearing a logo. I'm still trying to understand the objective satisfaction people get from it. Whatever it is, it works. When stars wear brands, we want to be like them. But feeling our best comes from being ourselves, certainly not from wearing a brand.

Marketing is the nemesis of the rational mind. There is nothing reasonable about paying $75 or $100 for a T-shirt when it is disturbingly easy to have a quality T-shirt custom-made for less.

Brands are also a means of social acceptance, a sort of insurance policy against rejection. Buying the same brand as a group of friends is the equivalent of putting your trust in a certain segment of the population.

I remember a university accounting course I taught. To liven it up, I would ask students questions, but rather than calling them by name, I would call them by the brands they were wearing.

Mr. Apple or Ms. Michael Kors, can you answer the question?

Sometimes, I would pretend not to recognize the brand.

Yes, young man with the Ultramar shirt, can you answer the question?

It's not Ultramar; it's American Eagle!

Oh. It looks like an Ultramar shirt. Answer the question?

That's one way of negating the pride of wearing an expensive shirt: associate the luxury item with its opposite (in this case, a home fuel retailer). I enjoyed watching them make fun of their lame professor who didn't know the first thing about the hottest brands. The students, who were in their early twenties, were surprised, and then incredulous. They were stunned that their teacher's world didn't include what they considered to be of most value at that moment. And they couldn't understand how I was unmoved by logos.

Did my jokes really make them think? I don't think so. But when you plant a seed, you have to water it. With watering, I told myself the idea would end up sprouting.

Yesterday's desire and tomorrow's junk

Over the years, brands come and go and fashion changes, but the principle remains. One year it was Burton, another it was Tommy Hilfiger. And of course there was the Canada Goose coat, a virtual uniform. In the corridors of the business school HEC Montréal, it was practically a joke. **Seeing so many students buy $600 winter coats is like seeing Georges Laraque on a power play for the Canadiens: it's a curious allocation of resources.** Remember Vuarnet T-shirts? They have pretty much disappeared from the fashion landscape, except for a few that are in good-enough shape for a Salvation Army rack.

Another example of the phenomenon is tablets and computers. Who really needs a Mac at university? If you are a graphic designer or in a particular field, you may be able to justify it, but it's fascinating to see the number of people who buy a MacBook Pro for word processing. Seriously? Aside from showing off the little apple in class and creating a sense of belonging, does it help the student write an assignment faster? Most students could make do with a $600 computer, but they want more. Why? Because it's more attractive?

There was a time when computers were beige and ugly, but that didn't matter—what people wanted from a computer was performance. Times have changed, but the purpose of the machine remains the same. The problem is that we are being sold a sense of belonging as well as the brand design. This is the sense of belonging logos create.

Apple users aren't just consumers; they're disciples. Disciples who want to hear the annual high mass when new products come out. Disciples prepared to defend the brand and be complicit in planned obsolescence. **Score one for marketing.**

Another example of marketing-generated desire is guitars. I long dreamed of owning a Gretsch, a Gibson or a Fender Telecaster. Why? Because international musicians are walking billboards for these sound-generating, tuned planks of wood. Every time a camera shows a musician playing a solo, it zooms in on the guitar. When a musician changes instruments during a show, it draws attention to the guitar and reinforces the brand presence.

I've always dreamed about an expensive guitar, but is my talent worth the $3,000 investment? Not a chance. Even if my talent justified it, do I make my living playing music? No. So why do I need an exclusive brand of guitar? Because agreements between musicians and manufacturers make us want what the big boys play.

If Bruce Springsteen plays a particular guitar, it becomes a symbol of good ol' American rock 'n' roll.

Brands project us into someone else's appealing reality. The brain makes an association, but it also lacks critical judgment when it comes to lending meaning to our interpretation of brands. When a star is associated with a product, does it make sense? Are they endorsing the product, or do they just want the cheque? Does Eugenie Bouchard really guzzle Diet Coke?

Sometimes the brand values are out of step with reality. Take tennis player Maria Sharapova. She says she takes drugs to prevent diabetes, which runs in her family. But she has her own brand of candies, Sugarpova. It makes you wonder . . .

Athletes and public personalities associate themselves with brands even when their expertise and behaviour have nothing to do with the product. Yet somehow our brains accept this sort of contradiction. If Sharapova were to endorse a tennis racket company, that would make a lot more sense than candy.

Being aware of our weakness

Brands leave their mark on our brains. It's smoke and mirrors. We know it; we feel it. We can't explain why we become slaves to them. We are suffering from a cognitive bias of representativeness. The more positive comments you hear about a brand, the more your brain attributes value to it. So we just need to be aware of it.

On the other hand, some brands are so rooted in our unconscious that they are like a tattoo and become part of our thought process. We no longer choose a product among readily available brands; we demand ONE brand, for which we have a favourable cognitive predisposition. It is hard to break free of the reflex of choosing a name or luxury brand, even if the price difference is substantial.

Want proof?

Why not buy the generic of a drug when the ingredients are exactly the same as the original advertised on TV?

Why buy one brand of spring water over another? Is there really a difference in taste? Why buy bottled bubbly water from the other side of the planet rather than one from a local spring?

Why buy any salt other than the cheapest one? S-A-L-T: NaCI! $?!?!$ Since when can two combined elements from the periodic table be differentiated? *Yes, but it's sea salt!* Give me a break. (My editor tells me she prefers Maldon salt on her tomatoes. I've promised her I will try it.)

Buying a product based on brand is admitting our weakness. Sure, consumers may like certain products and buy a brand by default and not for the prestige. But it has become hard to imagine a world without brands. Even nature has brands. Geographical areas have brands. Everything is a brand. If things keep going this way, a certain Montreal hockey executive may start calling himself TradeMarc Bergevin.

Any adult living in a consumer society will have their judgment impaired by brand recognition.

A brand is a promise of quality, prestige, service, reliability and trust.

A brand is what a company is trying to build through its reputation or through advertising.

Yes, a brand image may be associated with value, but is that the real reason we buy the associated products?

So do you really need brands? No. But if you have ample savings, go ahead and splash out. Because splashing out and living life to the fullest means wearing designer labels (#sarcasm). Plus they give you a certain cachet (#moresarcasm).

NEGOTIATING
DO YOU REALLY NEED IT?

L ife is one long negotiation. Negotiation is ubiquitous and eternal. And it starts early: children are negotiating champions. It's in their blood, particularly when it comes to staying up later.

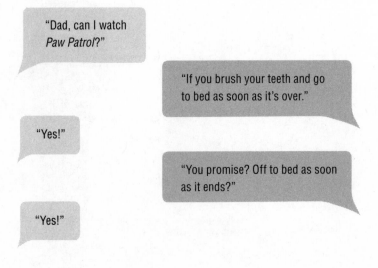

"Dad, can I watch *Paw Patrol*?"

"If you brush your teeth and go to bed as soon as it's over."

"Yes!"

"You promise? Off to bed as soon as it ends?"

"Yes!"

Obviously, this is when I know I've lost the negotiation. Why? Because I have no leverage if he throws a tantrum after the movie. If he refuses to go to bed, I can punish him in a variety of ways. But I won't have control over the only thing I want: the peace and quiet I need to work tonight. So, after a little over an hour, the inevitable happens . . .

"Okay, the show's over. Time for bed."

"That's not fair. I didn't get to play. I don't wanna go to bed."
(Doing his best imitation of Grouchy Smurf.)

"Édouard, you promised."
(In the tone of a father who thinks he can negotiate rationally with a child of four and a half.)

"WAAAAAAAAAAAAAAAAAAAAAAAAHHHHHHHHHHHH!"

"Go to bed!"

"Will you read me a story?"
(Pitiful tone.)

"Get into bed and I'll read you a story."

And that's how my son just bought himself a free extension on the contract. The contract was to go to bed, but he wants a bit more. He uses his leverage; he knows that I want him to go to sleep and that, ultimately, he's the one, fearing no punishment, who has the upper hand.

I'm tired. I'll do anything for some peace and quiet, and the house is too small for a tantrum. Afterwards, he'll use the classic final request strategy:

> "Can I have a glass of water?"

Two minutes later:

> "Can you rub my belly?"
> (My son thinks he's a dog.)

Five minutes later:

> "You didn't sing me my song!"
> (Because, obviously, "Frère Jacques" is his and his alone.)

Finally, he gets the better of the enemy by wearing him down. In other words, my son used the strategy of **asking for one last thing before closing the transaction.**

It's a simple thing for negotiating buyers. When you are negotiating with a salesperson, just before finalizing the transaction, ask for one last trifling thing. It has to be tiny compared with the total amount of the purchase. The salesperson will give it to you to avoid losing the sale.

For example, you're shopping for a $5,000 above-ground pool. Before you shake the salesperson's hand, you say,

> "I'll buy it right now if you throw in the winter pool cover."

You know it's not a deal-breaker, but it's still a hundred dollars you won't have to shell out later. For the salesperson, it isn't worth it to risk losing the sale for such a paltry amount, so generally he or she will give it to you.

When salespeople act like advisers and friends, they are like hunters setting out the bait when they have the deer in their sights. Lovely though they may be, salespeople are never truly advisers; they are transaction specialists. When they shake your hand, inside they are jumping for joy: they have just made money.

I don't hold it against salespeople who want to sell. It's their job. I am the prey; they are the predator. What remains is whether I let them walk all over me or I get one up on them.

Every step in a negotiation is a game. To do well, you just have to play.

Reading the salesperson's strategy

Sometimes, salespeople will use the classic strategy of the **false dilemma** to close a transaction.

> "So, are you going to take the signature guitar or the custom model?"

The consumer is being backed into the buyer's corner. He came in to look around and to think, and the salesperson isn't giving him a chance to, because he wants him to buy. So the conversation turns toward the transaction: the choice to be made. The consumer, who may be uncomfortable, is rushed into making a purchase. An innocent but consenting victim of the trumped-up dilemma, he is backed into the corner of the immediate purchase. He lost, the salesperson won. I use this strategy often with my son.

> "Édouard, do you want to wear this shirt or that one?"

> "Do you want to go to the Biodome or the park?"

And it works. It's child's play.

Protecting yourself

Another sales strategy is called **the trap**. The customer is a black box. Walking into a store, you are judged on your appearance, attitude, how much of a hurry you are in, and so on.

But a great deal of information about you is not available to the salesperson. So when you hesitate, salespeople try to get information from you. They set a trap by asking: "What would influence your choice?" If you answer honestly, you have lost and fallen into the trap.

If price is the issue, the salesperson will suggest something less expensive. If quality is the concern, the salesperson will go for the top of the line. And once you offer up information, they'll have you right where they want you. Because a sale is a decision tree: every piece of information leads to the close—the right transaction for the right consumer. What I call a trap could also be called advice. But a true adviser would actually ask, "Do you really need it?"

The rookie mistake that you shouldn't make in a negotiation is the **anchoring bias**. The first one who names a price has lost. For example, when I tell my son, "If you're good, maybe we'll go to the Biodome," I've just let him know that I'm prepared to go to the Biodome. This information is anchored in his brain: today, Dad is prepared to go as far as the Biodome; he has committed, and we can go as far as there. The same principle applies in negotiation.

Rest assured that if your answer to the question "What's your budget?" is $30,000, you will be offered a price right around there or slightly higher, even if a lower-range, more affordable product would have suited you. You revealed your limit . . . why shouldn't the salesperson take advantage of it?

It reminds me of a trendy restaurant on St-Laurent Boulevard I went to with my spouse. The waiter arrived. The classic: twenty-five to twenty-eight years old with facial hair that would put Colonel Sanders to shame. Behold: the hipster. He didn't smile, because that would remove some of his mystery. He had a whiff of an international accent, even though he probably grew up in a working-class neighbourhood in the city.

He got straight to the anchoring bias strategy. I asked about a white wine my boss served in his catering business. He checked and told me the wine wasn't on the list. But he could suggest a similar white that would pair well with what we had ordered.

"Around how much did you want to spend?"

"Around $60." (Which is already three times the price of the same wine at the liquor store.)

"I have something in mind. I'll be right back."

He goes to the cellar and comes back.

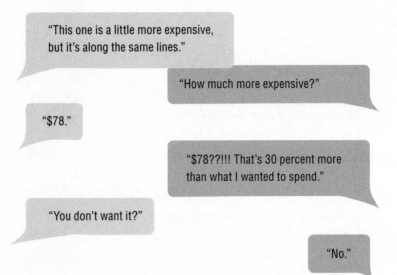

"This one is a little more expensive, but it's along the same lines."

"How much more expensive?"

"$78."

"$78??!!! That's 30 percent more than what I wanted to spend."

"You don't want it?"

"No."

My tone was curt. The waiter wanted to take advantage of the fact that the average customer feels uncomfortable declining a bottle because of the price. However, it doesn't bother me in the slightest. I know my limit, and I didn't really need that bottle. But the waiter knew full well that upping the ante by $18 would give him at least $3 more in a tip, with no more effort. No matter the price of the wine, his job was the same.

"This one is very good. It's $52."

Using the anchoring bias strategy, the waiter had tried to sell me a bottle $26 more expensive than the one I ended up choosing. Implicitly, we were engaged in a negotiation. Of course, we didn't negotiate on the price; we just negotiated on the right bottle for my needs.

In the wide range of sales strategies, there is also the infamous **"I have to check with my boss."** It's a pantomime I love to watch. The goal is simple: to get customers to believe that they have reached the outer limit of what can be negotiated.

The strategy is meant to stroke the customer's ego. Often, the boss comes to see the customer with the salesperson to talk and show that this is a special case. It's actually nothing of the sort; it's common practice. The goal is to try to maximize gross margin. If the customer likes to negotiate, the merchant adjusts. **When shopping, if you do not ask, ye shall not receive.**

Case in point: One of my friends talked down the price of a breast pump at a Jean Coutu drugstore. She got to the cash and asked to see the manager. In a few minutes she had a 10 percent discount on the pump. Who would have thought to try to negotiate at a big drugstore chain? Obviously, you can't do it for everything, but for expensive products that don't sell every day, the manager may want to reduce inventory.

Ending the game

The biggest risk for the salesperson is not selling, and the biggest risk for the buyer is overpaying. So, postponing your purchase often makes sense.

Don't be afraid to act as though you're indifferent about a product or service. Negotiate, but remember that if you make a mistake, you have the option of leaving the store and coming back better prepared on another day. **The wisest purchases are often the ones we don't make.**

Life is one long series of negotiations. Just think of your career. We tend to forget, but a salary and position in a company is the result of negotiation. We negotiate our salary to increase our income, and we negotiate our purchases to minimize spending.

So negotiation affects both the revenue and expense columns. Financial leeway is the result of a multitude of negotiations. The negotiation game is ubiquitous. Don't like playing? Your personal finances wish you did.

Basically, you have to be rich not to negotiate. Every time you enter into a transaction without negotiating, you subsidize those who know how to play the game. So, do you have the means not to negotiate?

COMFORT
DO YOU REALLY NEED IT?

"... the lust for comfort, that stealthy thing that enters the house a guest, and then becomes a host, and then a master."
— KAHLIL GIBRAN, "On Houses"

Many of our economic choices are influenced by the quest for comfort. Why take the car to run an errand less than a kilometre away instead of going by bike? So you don't get hot, to minimize effort and to save time (which isn't necessarily the case)—in short, for greater comfort.

Safety is part of psychologist Abraham Maslow's "hierarchy of needs," frequently shown as a pyramid. In today's world, we could probably put the need for comfort on that pyramid, along with esteem, belongingness and self-actualization.

In fact, when we live comfortably, it's as though we become one with our needs.

We build a life; we acquire what we think are basic goods: a washing machine, a car and a home. Then we start wanting to be as comfortable as others.

The minute you walk into someone's house, the comparisons start. Are they more comfortable than me? An unconscious—or conscious—part of our brain is affected. Friends are like Blue Jays fans: they're more than happy to be walking billboards for consumer society.

When we have people over, we like to point out the pool or the sofa we've just bought. As if the sum of what we buy creates social standing. **The greater the comfort, the more self-esteem we have**: we admire the comfort we have bought for ourselves, as if achieving it was an accomplishment in and of itself.

Comfort is part of a universal goal. In a society where we no longer need to fight to survive, we have chosen a more superficial fight: whether pursuing new foodie heights or stuffing our faces with junk food, admiring the leather in a new car or enjoying the oh-so-comforting look of others admiring us, we desire a certain level of comfort.

Eventually, we forget what discomfort is. We lose the habit of effort, sacrifice, investment and striving. We wind up saying, "This is how I am, and it is what it is." Eventually, the quest for comfort and happiness without sacrifice becomes our loss.

The comfort drug: the quest for inertia

Paying attention to your personal finances carries with it an opportunity cost. Earning extra income requires ongoing effort, just as cutting expenses does.

It's more fun to eat a sandwich at the bakery surrounded by people than to make a sandwich alone at home. Similarly, it's easier to veg in front of the TV every night rather than go out for a thirty-minute jog.

Comfort is a drug that calls to us like a sugar craving. It's responsible for some dubious economic choices.

Always replacing things awakens another type of comfort in us: the comfort of being at the leading edge. We refuse to fall out of fashion. It's as though the mind is calmed by being up to date. We keep searching for the latest thing, as if it were a way of staying young or aging more slowly.

Seeking comfort doesn't only wreak havoc on your wallet; it gets imprinted in the mind and creates inertia. Then eventually, in the name of comfort, we don't want to change: we stagnate on our improvement curve. We reach a summit, a first derivative that equals zero on the continuous improvement curve (one for the nerds out there).

Comfort in love

On the road to pleasure, love is no exception. A comfortable, well-established love life eliminates the desire to start over again. The discomfort of a dissatisfying but stable relationship is sometimes the lesser evil, compared with the uncertainty and pain of a breakup.

Similarly, sometimes there is less discomfort in ending a relationship that has just begun than in investing in it. Compromise can be a source of displeasure; achieving perfection is impossible, and the search for it creates varying levels of well-being. The more comfort plunges us into inertia, the more we are wary of compromise, sharing our life and evolving.

Constant comparison

Fighting to create a place for yourself and using sustained effort to achieve your goals is easily judged by others. We compare levels of comfort. Rather than saying, "She works too much," our brain rewords it to say, "She is ready to accept a lot more discomfort than I am."

This brings us to the notion of envy. We envy the other person's ability to sustain and accept discomfort, because the inertia in our own mind isn't prepared to tolerate such a comfort gap. Denying opportunity to maintain a satisfactory level of comfort becomes a reflex.

Our relationship with the environment is also driven by this need for comfort. We can be eco-friendly as long as we don't have to make any extra effort to be more responsible. We are happy to put a plastic bottle in the recycling bin, but only if a bin is available, and we do it to avoid the inconvenience of carting the bottle home to recycle it.

Or say you want to buy an electric car, for the psychological comfort of making a green choice. However, it costs more to buy one, which creates substantial discomfort. (But are we really reducing energy consumption? Not entirely, because the green option still consumes energy when it is manufactured and used. Energy is a scarce resource, and even if there may be less of an environmental impact, there is one regardless.)

The same thing applies to showers: we would rather waste hot water than soap up with the water off. We trade off having water run needlessly for several minutes for the pleasant feeling of warmth.

Similarly, we heat our homes two degrees higher than necessary because it's nice to wear short sleeves in the winter.

And just think of the popularity of remote car starters, a product of the comfort society. **In the wake of the consumer society, we have achieved the comfort society.**

Then there is the bizarre desire to possess a lot of things. We accumulate stuff to perform tasks that we do only rarely. Once a certain level of comfort has been achieved, you end up in the ridiculous situation of being a collector.

Collecting things, in addition to keeping the mind occupied, fills a void. It's tangible proof of the time we spend on something, a way of lending colour to our existence.

Comfortable and happy work?

Like relationships, work can become a source of comfort or discomfort. A regular job with a decent salary can be an obstacle to taking the risk of seeking greater career fulfillment.

On the flip side, what if you have a job you love that doesn't pay the rent?

Professionally, you have to pile up the discomforts of risk, work, overtime, skills development and self-promotion to ultimately figure out your "value" in the marketplace.

Let's take the example of a permanent employee in the public service with a defined contribution pension plan. Before considering making a move, he whips out the calculator. If he can count, he will see that after ten or fifteen years' service, he shouldn't move to another job, because the opportunity cost would be too great.

A defined contribution plan pays off only if you reach retirement age while still on the job. The euphoria of considering new challenges and professional achievement is traded in for the quiet certainty of a job that comes with slippers.

But this creates a paradox: staying in a job offers the reassurance of a salary, but often prevents people from experiencing something better because they don't give themselves a chance.

So, when it comes to personal finances, you have to go through a period of discomfort to achieve comfort. You need to build your net assets to attain financial leeway. Unless you inherit a lot of money or enjoy unusually high financing for the middle class, eventually you find yourself in discomfort. You have to learn to live with it and even appreciate it.

At some point, discomfort can become a source of motivation, because you know you will learn to adapt, and fast. Comfort is related to the concept of managing expectations (see "Managing Expectations: Do You Really Need To?" on page 248). If you get too used to comfort, you may throw in the towel at the slightest sign of discomfort.

Comfort can therefore be the goal, or it can be a check on ambition. One thing is certain: the quest for comfort (or maintaining it) can put obstacles on the path to happiness. In a sense, I am, we are, you are and they are slaves to the objective of becoming comfortably dumb. Now that would be a great adaptation of the Pink Floyd song.

Has your budget stopped balancing?

Are your dreams buried deep inside?

Can you reduce your need for comfort? Do you really need it?

Not asking yourself questions can be an insidious way of comforting yourself. But consumer debt is !%#*?& uncomfortable when you're in search of freedom. *Carpe diem.* (Provided your retirement account is in good shape.)

!%#*?& POINTS CARDS
DO YOU REALLY NEED THEM?

One of the most pointless, ridiculous arguments I've ever had with my partner was about points cards.

I remember it well. On our way home after a night out, my partner mentioned that we needed gas. At that point, we were close to home and a Petro-Canada station.

Seeing where I was heading, she said, "No, go to the Shell station!" Um, why go somewhere else? It's gas. It's not as if the car we had at the time, a magnificent Chrysler Neon held together by rust, had a discriminating palate.

Nearing the 200,000-kilometre mark, the car was like a centenarian, half asleep, blowing out the candles on another birthday cake. Every extra kilometre required an effort that was pushing it closer to the end of its useful life. So, why go to Shell?

My spouse spoke the words as malodorous as anything that can emerge from my sons' digestive tracts: "We'll earn Air Miles."

After losing my patience trying to explain the trifling return we would get from this absurd detour, I gave in because I just wanted to go home to bed (and with the discussion we had just had, I could forget any other ideas I had for the evening). So I drove from Rachel Street to Sherbrooke Street, a distance of 1.1 kilometres, just to go to the Shell station.

Once there—yippee!—after making the detour for the *!%#*?& Air Miles, sometime after 10 p.m. on a winter's night, we noticed that—could it get any more ridiculous?—a litre of gas cost *more* than at Petro-Canada. So, for a few thousand Air Miles, not only had we argued over peanuts, but we had overpaid for forty litres of gas. Basically, a stupid marketing ploy had cost me precious minutes of my life.

Here's the thing: the discounts with the Air Miles programme are infinitesimal. You practically have to fork out the equivalent of the value of a car to get a free blender. When my spouse gives me a "Triple your reward miles with any purchase" coupon, I feel as though she's just given me a coupon that says, "Triple your peanuts."

Loyalty building and big data

We know for a fact that points are a marketing ploy used to generate loyalty among customers and to enable merchants to profile consumer habits. We also know that if we don't take part, we still pay the price for those who do.

There is a **cardinal rule: spending money to earn points is moronic.** (To be clear, I'm not talking about credit card points, but "free" loyalty points with store cards.)

What's more, points cards turn your wallet into a six-drawer filing system. With all the chain stores with their own loyalty programmes, you end up with a card for every grocery store, drugstore, hardware store, clothing store and so on. This is on top of the cards that any citizen or parent has to carry. (At least smartphones will eventually solve at least part of the problem of accumulating cards.)

We are a long way from the days when I used to go outside, a key hanging around my neck, no wallet, money or ID. Childhood was the last bastion of freedom.

At any rate, one thing is certain: we have never been so spied upon as we are now. When you use points cards, you are leaving your trace everywhere. It's the trade-off we accept as customers: giving up our information in exchange for treats. A big brother of marketing is watching us, compiling data and profiling us with every transaction.

Why all the accumulation of data? To build loyalty among customers, to attract them and to sell to them. Retail operations no longer sell just products; they sell consumers who are buyers of products and services. You can attract them with a loss leader and get them to buy other products at a higher margin. For the sake of accumulating points, the customer will return rather than going to the competition.

Points cards trap us in a marketing system we are forced to participate in under penalty of leaving a financial return on the table. So, docile little sheep that we are, we trade our lives for a few dollars.

Concrete examples

Businesses like David's Tea have a points card for which any balance below 100 points is wiped out every December 31 if you don't use it to buy products. Basically, they force customers to return regularly to buy from their store to take advantage of their points.

You have to spend $100 on tea to get a free 50 grams. But the customer has to realize that "all free tea rewards expire 60 days after they are issued to you."[1] And the company knows that when customers come in to get their free tea, they will be tempted to buy a little more.

The goal is always to attract customers back to the store and persuade them not to shop at the competition. Plus, since tea is a differentiated product,[2] it is hard for customers to compare prices between stores.

And anyway, it's not the price that is sold to the customer; it's the flavour. It's only at the cash that customers realize the cost. But they are still happy to pay for their overpriced tea because they will get free tea in three months. It's not a gift; they are just encouraging the customer to pay in advance.

A little while ago, even the Société des alcools du Québec (SAQ) introduced a loyalty programme. That took some nerve.

The SAQ is a monopoly in Quebec. Sorry, a virtual monopoly, because low-grade wine is sold in grocery stores and convenience stores. What could be better than a nice white Caballero de Chile to unclog your kitchen sink or get the stains out of a shirt? (Please forgive my gratuitous cynicism, but it feels good.)

The programme, called Inspire, doesn't inspire me at all. At the SAQ, they aren't allowed to call it a loyalty programme, but the economic fundamentals are the same: the more you consume, the more points you earn.

---

1   https://www.davidstea.com/ca_en/faq/frequent-steeper/

2   This is a product to which value is added by marketing, or by features or other objective or subjective differences. By promoting differentiation, two sorts of tea will not be considered identical by all consumers.

You essentially pay for the programme through the wine you buy during the year. They say the programme is meant to better target customer needs. Oh, really? To my way of thinking, the customer's real need is to get advice and a good wine at the right price.

The SAQ awards five points for every dollar spent. You need to spend $200 to get $1 in rewards. So if you buy 100 bottles at $20 each, you get a free half bottle.

For a free $10 bottle, you have to drink about two $20 bottles a week for a year. Obviously, you can take advantage of featured products and earn more points. Therein lies the rub: they will recommend bottles I will supposedly like, but they will also push featured products down my throat through points.

Basically, gone are the days of instant discounts on bottles. They are being replaced with another points system. I prefer the days when the SAQ offered a 10 or 15 percent discount on purchases of $100 or more. That way I could do my buying for three months at a reduced price. When I remember those days, the Inspire programme looks more like the Despair programme.

This chapter is a tirade against points programmes that are based on the frequency and amount of products consumed. It seems it's too hard for companies to distinguish themselves by offering good service and good products at the right price.

The only way to fight points systems is to consume less and go to local stores where the added value may not require a loyalty programme.

The next time someone mentions points, I'm going to get in the shower, curl up in a ball and stay there for a week. Because do I really need !%#?& points cards?

HIGH-END EQUIPMENT
DO YOU REALLY NEED IT?

It's always surprising to see someone work themselves to the bone to buy high-end equipment. Most people can't afford it.

High-end products are put on this earth to make us dream, to make us believe that we deserve them. There is a world of difference between deserving and desiring. Deserving goes beyond desiring: it's object worship.

A clarification to begin with

It is easy to confuse high-end with quality. You can own an affordable, quality item that isn't necessarily luxury or high-end. Basically, the item is well made, and it costs more than something that is disposable, maybe, because it is associated with a brand or marketing campaign or is just exclusive.

When you buy something, you should be buying quality, not status. High-end equipment is often good quality, but it is meant for experts, professionals and true aficionados.

High-end equipment is expensive and not necessarily what you really need. But buying crap is expensive too, because you end up having to buy it again.

The word to keep in mind when shopping is *durable*. You want to buy durable goods without falling into the status trap. As I mentioned in "Brands: Do You Really Need Them?" (page 23), a Louis Vuitton bag is high-end luxury. But do the bag's quality and durability reflect the price? Not necessarily.

Classic examples

Bikes are a good example. Members of a local cycling club aren't going to compete in the Tour de France, nor are they going to earn their living racing. But they like cycling so much that paying $5,799 plus tax to bike in the summer somehow makes sense to them. I'm always astonished by what people will pay for bikes.

 "But it's carbon!" I predict it won't be long before bike shops will be selling cyclists carbon water bottles, carbon shoes and carbon helmets.

In 1994, I bought a new bike. It took me a long time to save the $534 I needed to buy a red Giant Perigeé. It may not have been top-of-the-line, but it was a quality bike at the time.

Every year for the past ten years, I have visited a bike store. I've been tempted by a road bike the salesperson presented as "lower mid range" . . . for $2,000. Every time, I go home to avoid giving in to impulse (see "A Spending Strategy: Do You Really Need It?" on page 243). I let myself come down from the excitement of considering a purchase. I ask myself, "Pierre-Yves, do you really need it?" And then I keep riding my old road bike for another year.

When you get into high-end stereo systems, we're talking total decadence. You decide to set up an audio room to house a stereo system that costs tens of thousands of dollars, and a special chair for your listening pleasure.

But by the time you finally have the money you need to buy the whole set-up, you've probably lost your hearing. And what's the point of buying equipment if you can't even tell it is better quality?

These questions can apply to cars, ski equipment, furniture and more. What's going on in our heads that makes us want to buy things that are more than we need? Why are we drawn to increasingly luxurious, high-end equipment? It's a mystery.

What I do know is that owning something is not an achievement; it's just a fact. I don't become somebody because I dropped $20,000 on the latest McIntosh amplifier.

> ## FREE TIP!
>
> The magazine *Consumer Reports* does objective testing on consumer goods. Before buying something, find an independent source of information that reviews the product you are looking for. It will steer you in the right direction.

So why keep dreaming of high-end equipment? Does it make us better people? If that's what we think, we may be due for a visit to the psychologist. High-end equipment: do you really need it?

A BUDGET
DO YOU REALLY NEED IT?

You know something's wrong. You don't feel well. You go see the doctor, and she thumps your chest and asks you to say "ahhhh." She tells you to take a deep breath. She takes your blood pressure. She weighs you and sticks a cold stethoscope on your chest.

But you know what you have. You just want antibiotics for your sinusitis or urinary tract infection. So why does the doctor need to do a general checkup? So she can bill for one more medical procedure, of course, but that's not what we're talking about here. The doctor is looking for symptoms of what ails you, and will then zero in on the causes and propose a solution: a treatment, a drug—maybe even a prescription for exercise.

When it comes to our health, we react when symptoms appear. We see the doctor, change our behaviour or find a solution to fix it.

We should be taking the same attitude when our personal finances are under the weather. There's only one remedy: making a budget. But this is when we tend to go into denial, the ultimate avoidance tool.

59

When the family finances go off course

Your accounts don't balance, your credit card balance is climbing, and you are deep into your line of credit. Month by month, you're sinking. You can't sleep, and you feel uneasy every time you take your wallet out.

Like the pea that prevented the princess from sleeping, your precarious finances are wreaking havoc with your rest, no matter how many mattresses of denial they are buried under. You know you've got something, but you're afraid to find out just what.

So you try to forget, but the symptoms persist. You know what's at the root of the problem: you're spending more than you make. You're in debt. And it snuck up on you. You thought you could get a handle on it, but things are getting out of control.

You have to face it: you need to make a BUDGET (a nod to MARIE-CHANTAL TOUPIN, AND ALL THE OTHER PEOPLE WHO LIKE WRITING IN CAPITALS). No, anything but that! Make me wash diapers, force me to run 10 K a day, put me on a sugar-free, salt-free, taste-free diet, but don't tell me I need to make a budget!

But you can't use a rag to drive a nail. **A budget is the hammer in your financial tool box: the basic, universal tool.** It lets you hit the right expenses and investments and rip out bad habits.

The budget: your blood pressure monitor

A budget is a tool for monitoring the health of your finances. It boils down to a few lines that show various spending categories. For each line, you need to set a budget for a given period. Then, at the end of the period, you add up the actual amount you spent and try to justify the difference.

Make sure you have a line for expenses that don't occur regularly. For example, if your youngest has teeth like Austin Powers, it may be a good idea to set aside a little every month to pay for the orthodontist when the time comes.

Having enough for major expenses and long-term investments helps you build a lasting budget.

Excerpt from a budget for September 2016

ITEM	ACTUAL	BUDGET	VARIANCE	EXPLANATION
Restaurants	$500	$400	+$100	François's birthday not planned for.
Hair stylist	$100	$60	+$40	I needed highlights!
Clothing	$600	$300	+$300	My Canada Goose coat will last.
Birthday gifts	$0	$100	-$100	My husband lacked ambition. I left him a week before his birthday.

The four budget lines show that an extra $440 was spent for the month, and an anticipated expenditure of $100 was avoided. So, in the monthly budget, these lines are responsible for overspending of $340. What do you do to balance? Where do you cut? "Nowhere" is not an option for most people. Unless you can boost your income substantially, you need to make some adjustments.

Yes, you can work on the income side. But it's taxable. If your marginal tax rate (the tax rate on the next dollar earned above a predefined income threshold) is 37.12 percent (on actual income of $50,000 per year), that means you have to earn an extra $159.03 to pay for $100 in spending. Increasing your income can be a solution, but will it create a major imbalance? (see "Balance: Do You Really Need It?" on page 91).

Playing both sides of the equation is also an option: increasing your income *and* reducing your expenses. According to Equifax, Canadians' average consumer debt for the last quarter of 2017 was $22,837,[1] which includes car payments, credit cards, lines of credit and other types of personal loans. This debt obviously excludes a mortgage.

Tools to help you

To create a budget that works, you need to identify every expenditure. Financial institution websites have tools for doing this.

The Quebec-based credit union Desjardins offers an interesting and comprehensive dynamic PDF file.[2] When you look at the list of items it includes, you start to understand how many different sources of incoming and outgoing funds there are for the average family. Be forewarned: when you first open the file, it may make your head spin.

 You can also check your bank statements (accounts and credit cards) to figure out what you are spending your money on. That way, you can quantify each line item based on past behaviour.

1   www.consumer.equifax.ca/about-equifax/press-releases/-/blogs/total-canadian-consumer-debt-climbs-to-over-1-8-trillion-but-delinquencies-and-bankruptcies-edge-down

2   www.desjardins.com/wcm/idc/documents/e35-budget-e.pdf

Making a budget

In companies, administration involves four major activities, summed up by the initialism PODC: planning, organizing, directing and controlling. This method can also apply to the family budget.

To understand the concept, let's take the example of spaghetti sauce (my teaching colleague likes to explain this sort of thing using what interests him: cooking).

> **P**: Make a list of ingredients and plan when to go to the grocery store.
> **O**: Get the ingredients ready, and organize tasks, e.g., chopping vegetables.
> **D**: Get things going by turning on the stove and combining ingredients.
> **C**: Taste while it cooks to adjust seasonings if needed.

So let's take that logic and apply it to making a budget.

Planning
- ✔ Establish the budget.
- ✔ Decide on the line items and amounts.
- ✔ Answer the following questions: How much do I want to save every month? How should I do that? And so on.

Organizing
- ✔ What tasks do I need to accomplish during the month?
- ✔ Who manages payments? How and when? (For example, it could be by transferring funds from a personal to a joint account on a specific date.)
- ✔ Which types of expenditures are acceptable and which aren't?
- ✔ Who will prepare meals? On what day? What is that person's responsibility for the monthly budget?

Directing
- ✔ Track bills, make payments.
- ✔ Make monthly decisions as to whether or not an expense is necessary.
- ✔ Monitor bank account to manage cash flow.

Controlling

The essential step of the budget is controlling. If you don't check that your budget balances at the end of the month, you can't correct habits or rethink decisions.

Think of someone who wants to lose weight, weighs himself, decides to go on a diet and eats accordingly, but who doesn't check in the mirror or on the scale to see whether the plan is working. If it fails, he will have to go back to the planning stage.

Basically, if your budget doesn't balance at the end of the month, there may be a few reasons.

- ✔ **An error in your estimates.** You forgot that a lot of friends have birthdays this month (planning).

✔ **Poorly understood responsibilities.** For instance, you forgot to make dinner and the solution was to order in (organizing). (See "Cooking: Do You Really Need To?" on page 264.)

✔ **Bad decisions.** Non-essential expenses were added, such as the impulse purchase of a $400 purse (directing). (See "Brands: Do You Really Need Them?" on page 23.)

✔ **Not balancing.** In comparing income and expenditures with the initial budget, you see that you spent more than you earned (controlling).

How do you change your habits?

My grandfather is from another era. To put together his budget, rather than creating an Excel spreadsheet, he uses a system of envelopes. Every time he gets paid, he distributes the money between the envelopes, which are identified by category: one for clothes, one for food, and so on.

Credit wasn't an option in his time, so he borrowed from himself. When he went over budget in one envelope, he drew from another. He didn't have a choice. Each additional child drained the envelopes a little more, until that child was old enough to contribute to the family finances.

Without going through all that hassle, paying for things with cash or by debit card for a month is an interesting way to re-create the envelope exercise: can you pay all of your bills with the cash that comes into your account? For example, if your net monthly pay is $2,000, is your cash outlay more than $2,000?

If you aren't using a credit card or a line of credit, you can't splash out since you're working with a finite balance in your bank account. The easiest way to be responsible, if the situation becomes critical, is to cut up your credit cards. *But my points! I won't earn any points! Oh no!* You need to read or reread without delay "!%#*?& Points Cards: Do You Really Need Them?" on page 49.

Budgeting: an ongoing exercise?
You don't need to drive yourself crazy, but keeping a budget for a certain period of time can change the way you spend. Once healthy spending habits have been established, you can redo the budget sporadically or as needed.

Budgets provide a reality check of how your little daily expenditures add up. If you don't make a budget, how do you know how much you can afford to pay for something? Go with your gut? Stick your finger outside and base your decisions on the way the wind is blowing? You may not even realize that the wind is being generated by you, suddenly accelerating on the highway.

FREE TIPS!

Budgeting is easier when you have good filing habits. Here are a few tips for managing the family's finances.

- *Don't spread yourself thin.* When you have all your finances at one financial institution, you retain your power of negotiation, and, most importantly, you limit the number of people involved. You have electronic access to all your accounts, credit cards and other services in one place.
- *Think ahead for taxes.* Every year, I put an oversized envelope in a file. Every receipt, statement, bill or other document for my tax return goes in the envelope as soon as I receive it. At the end of the year, I don't have to hunt down papers: everything is there.
- *Consider electronic files.* Microsoft, Google and other companies offer free storage space in the cloud. Obviously, some people will argue that companies like Google could spy on the contents of our e-mails and documents. The degree of privacy you need is a personal decision. One thing is certain: you need to make sure your personal financial data is stored securely—digital receipts, scanned bills and any other documents that you want to consult anywhere, any time.

  With my cellphone, I now have access to a virtual home filing cabinet. Buying a two-sided scanner helps eliminate paper you don't need to keep.

Basically, a filing system is essential, particularly if you are self-employed with different sources of income, or own an income property.

Do you really need a budget if you stick to your original plan to contribute to your TFSA, your RRSP or your kids' RESP, while staying out of debt? Of course not.

But if you aren't contributing to such savings initiatives, you may be someone who could benefit from a budget.

We are often poorer than we think.

Try making a budget for one month just to see what it shows you. You may consider not buying new for a while (see "New Stuff: Do You Really Need It?" on page 152).

LISTENING TO OTHER PEOPLE
DO YOU REALLY NEED TO?

Other people. The ones who encourage us to do things, and then criticize and judge the things we do. We are all someone else's other. And it can be hard to figure out the motivations behind other people's comments, help and advice. Sometimes they want the best for us, but often they want to make themselves feel secure in their own choices, opportunities and way of seeing the world.

Whenever you make a choice that strays from the norm, you upset people without meaning to. Other people come in different forms, and we have different relationships with them—professional, friendly, romantic, sometimes tinged with hate and envy—that can clash when we come into contact. The realm of personal finances is no exception: others have an opinion on ours, and their opinion influences us.

One day, a friend said something that stuck in my head like a refrain from a song by La Compagnie Créole: "**What other people have takes nothing away from you.**" It may seem simple, but it points to something much deeper. My friend had detected envy in something I'd said during a conversation. Deep-green envy. We envy others for having a different life, a different reality, a different level of wealth. But why not concentrate on forging our own path and enjoying the journey?

On the twisting road of personal finances, imitating your neighbour is ill-advised. The term "personal finances" contains an important word: *personal*. Why? Because we don't live other people's lives: we don't have their luck, their physical appearance or their individual health concerns. We haven't had the same education or opportunities. Every life path creates a different financial reality.

So, judging other people's finances based on what they spend is missing the boat of the holistic approach. You need to have walked a mile in their shoes to understand their journey, their long-term needs, their comfort with risk, their personal reality and their financial profile. Focusing only on their spending can make you forget that they may have assets to sustain their purchases.

Others

The way we consume is clearly influenced by what others desire. When do we stop to ask ourselves if it's really what we want? **Why the constant consumption? To please others? To compare ourselves to others? To get along with others?** Freedom isn't just another word for nothing left to lose. It's the power to change your life.

Freedom is also the power to not end up in jail. It's hard to keep a healthy perspective in a world where there is constant pressure to spend, perform and excel. We seek out the extraordinary; we are no longer impressed by the merely ordinary.

For instance, spending a day in the great outdoors is disconcerting when we've grown accustomed to the urban world. There's nothing to buy out there. You have to find ways to have fun without buying beer. (Have you ever noticed that meeting up with people often involves an invitation to consume? We say, "Do you want to go for a beer?" or "Do you want to go out for dinner?" We are uncomfortable just saying, "Let's get together later," or "Do you want to go and get a glass of water?")

Our relationship with others encourages consumption, as if we're afraid of not having a goal, or as if we have to spend money to set the tone for an encounter.

Influences

I bought my casual winter jacket in January 2003. It still keeps me warm. It's still in good shape. But almost every time I wear it, someone says, "Wow, you still have your HEC Commerce Games jacket? How come?" Because it's still good. People don't like to hear that. They have owned four coats over the same period, because they "really needed them." The pull on a zipper is broken? Better get a new coat.

Even though my jacket doesn't look brand new, I keep it, out of conviction, and maybe a bit of stubbornness. I want to prove to myself that I'm not a slave to consumption for the sake of it. Without the judgment of others, I would have no reason to buy a new one. At thirty-eight years old, you stop caring what people think about how you dress. That may be why sometimes people laugh at how older people dress. But maybe they've figured it out. **Why throw something out when it's still good? Where does this extravagant desire to buy new things come from?**

For many of us, student years are lean years. I remember my truck-eating shoes at HEC Montréal,[1] and the sweater I wore too often. A classmate once said, "So you really like that sweater, eh?" He didn't understand where I came from. He couldn't. Going through university with two or three pairs of pants in rotation is a reality for many students. The concept of debt scared me as much as the plague.

Developing a thick skin about what others think isn't easy. Other people's perceptions influence our social value, our market value as an individual. Tell me what you wear, and I'll tell you the circles you run in.

As bizarre as it may seem, countless messages in pop culture reinforce the idea that it's almost better to live at your credit limit than to be called cheap.

Making choices

The thing is, making choices doesn't mean being cheap; it simply means you prefer to spend your money in other ways. So you might pay for a round of beer for your friends even as you keep wearing your old coat. You might drive an old car but take more expensive vacations or go out for dinner regularly.

No one can judge a lifestyle based on a single budget item. But haven't we all heard at one time or another, "Come on, you can afford it!" or "You work hard. Why don't you treat yourself a little?" But we are not others. The ability to live with serious financial stress varies from person to person.

---

1   In the popular TV show *Passe-Partout*, Passe-Montagne wore shoes that were split at either end. They ate up trucks like a president of the Treasury Board eats up leeway. At university, I didn't eat trucks, but I didn't have any leeway.

The advice of others is often Enemy Number One of personal finances. Listening to the cautious other will make us miss out on a profitable investment. The impulsive other will influence us to buy something that will tie our financial hands for months. The pragmatic other will tell it like it is but prevent us from dreaming of what's possible or playing the cards we have.

Beyond expected value (possible return multiplied by its probability),[1] sometimes there are opportunities that you have to know how to seize. And what about the jealous or envious others who would point to a path that leads away from our ambitions just to reassure themselves about their own choices?

What we are often missing is a forthright other. When we say, "I don't have a choice," someone who is frank can set us straight. Of course we have choices, particularly when it comes to personal finances.

Obviously, if you're living hand to mouth, your choices are few. Having less than $20,000 a year allows for subsistence, nothing more. **With such a low income, a few bad decisions can send us into a spiral of missed payments and debt for the rest of our days.**

People who say they don't have a choice are looking for approval. If they find it easily, they are reassured and maintain their lifestyle. To change, they need to be exposed to new ideas. Sometimes it takes hitting a wall—the one that allows them to be crushed by their creditors.

---

1   For example, if there is a 10 percent chance of making a gain of $1,000, the expected value is $100. The point is to calculate the statistical value of the potential return.

Dare to be yourself

For balance when it comes to other people's judgments, the key may be to spend time with people from different backgrounds. When you live in a friendship cocoon, you become like your Facebook account: your thinking algorithm is limited to the circle of people who eat, spend and live the same way you do.

Periodically immersing yourself in another social setting lets you appreciate what you have and opens your mind to other ways of managing your personal finances. **Social diversity is important: it allows us to aspire to be better and encourages awareness of our good fortune . . . or misery.**

In fact, the best other you can find is probably your balance sheet: your assets and debts set against your income and spending. We don't often consider that other. We systematically ignore it. It doesn't speak to love, feelings or impulsiveness. It's an imaginary being, but one that is frank, honest and pragmatic; it lets us check whether we can lighten up a little.

By definition, others are not us. They don't have to live with the consequences of our financial decisions. The greatest challenge to sound management of personal finances is to resist the temptation to live through the eyes of others or to let them define you.

Because the ultimate goal in life is to not end up in a public nursing home, with one sponge bath a week. It would be a shame if that were the outcome of a series of bad financial decisions, like having worn a $600 Canada Goose coat at age twenty-five or having listened to others. Because that, you really don't need.

A NEW CAR
DO YOU REALLY NEED IT?

I admit to having never understood people's obsession with cars. It probably has to do with my upbringing.

In 1983, my father had an old station wagon with faux wood side panels. He was never the type to maintain it, wash it or pamper it. When we drove through puddles, we had to lift our feet because the water splashed up through the holes in the floor. We were careful not to drop our change—because it would fall right through to the road.

Dad always said the car was just a heap of metal, but I thought he was unnecessarily negligent. There's a difference between not coddling your car and flat-out neglecting it.

My father took a narrowly utilitarian approach to car ownership. But as a society, we confuse the strict practicalities of driving with the burning desire to own a vehicle, defining ourselves by the car we drive.

How can we make a choice that is so hard on our finances without at least optimizing the return? Regardless of price, a car has to meet the primary requirement, which is getting us from point A to point B. Any other justification for such a purchase is about image, comfort, technology (see "The Latest Technology: Do You Really Need It?" on page 16), space and so on. **Basically, a large part of the value we attribute to cars has nothing to do with their primary function: getting around.**

Between desire and need

One day, a colleague who is single told me he wanted to buy a Jeep Grand Cherokee. I was curious, so I asked him why he wanted such a big vehicle. He pointed out how practical an SUV would be when he went fishing—once a year—with his father. I suggested he buy a smaller car for half the price and rent an SUV for that one week a year.

His justification fell apart . . . but his desire remained intact, and he searched for other reasons to convince himself that his intended purchase made sense. The desire to consume beats reason hands-down: when fantasizing over an object of desire, it is easy to twist your financial reasoning.

In our society, cars are probably one of the most poorly used expenditures (**an expenditure never delivers a return**). Are our financial resources optimized? Could we make a more rational financial choice?

And think about it: cars stay parked most of the time, monopolizing public space, depriving others of the ability to use it.

When I see cars permanently parked on the street, I sometimes ask myself, "What if we had a key that let us use any car at any time?" Given the demand, we would all have our needs met, at a much lower cost than individual car ownership. Maintenance costs could be shared as well, saving everyone time and money.

Instead, we all want to own our own car, and we identify with it, even though, as possessions go, it is expensive and inefficient.

For a fraction of the price, universal car sharing in urban centres could outweigh all the advantages of the personal car. It would be public transit, but for personal use. It could be the best of both worlds.

The fact test

A study published by CAA-Québec shows the extent to which owning and running a late-model car can be a major expense.[1] The actual cost of a car is underestimated by most drivers, whether consciously or unconsciously, a kind of defence mechanism.

For example, a Honda Civic LX, a very popular model in Canada, generates almost $6,500 annually in ownership costs for the first few years,[2] or a little under $18 a day for 18,000 kilometres travelled. This includes insurance, a driver's licence and registration, depreciation, and the average cost of financing.

This is in addition to the annual cost of running it, a little more than $2,600. When you add these two amounts together, the real annual cost is over $9,000 net.

A person with a salary of $50,000 takes home a net income of almost $39,000,[3] based on certain tax assumptions, such as including the basic personal tax credit. So, that person works 23 percent of his or her time during the year just to pay for a car, which is essentially used to . . . go to work.

---

[1]   www.caa.ca/wp-content/uploads/2012/06/CAA_Driving_Cost_French_2013_web-2.pdf

[2]   This is an average car. The more luxurious the car, the higher the cost.

[3]   http://www.ey.com/ca/en/services/tax/tax-calculators-2016-personal-tax

In other words, out of 2,000 hours (50 weeks) a year, you would have to work almost 11.5 weeks—a little over two months—just to pay the expenses for your rolling tin can.

According to Statistics Canada, the average Canadian household spends $11,909 annually for transportation. This adds up to 14 percent of total household spending, which was over $84,489 in 2016.[1]

When someone decides to buy a house far from their work, do they calculate the real cost, including transportation? Don't forget that when you buy a house, you recover the costs when you sell it—but the cost of transportation is never recovered. That means that living in the city near your work and giving up your car can save time and money.

A new car: value down the drain

I have never bought a new car; the price of a new car is disproportionate to its utility. The first three years are when you see the biggest drop in value (it's not unusual for average depreciation to

---

1   http://www.statcan.gc.ca/tables-tableaux/sum-som/l01/cst01/famil130a-eng.htm

be between 35 and 50 percent over thirty-six months). So, a $30,000 car would be worth less than $20,000 after three years. But it can run for many more years, particularly when lifestyle choices limit the number of kilometres you put on it every year.

So, new cars represent, on average, a higher cost per kilometre driven or per year of ownership. Driving a used car is one way not to tie yourself in financial knots.

In fall 2011, circumstances led me to make a quick decision to buy a beater: a shiny 1998 two-door Honda Accord, in aubergine. The price was $2,600, tax included. To my mind, this would get me through the year I needed it for. Then, as time went by, it always ended up making more financial sense to repair the car than to replace it.

Two years after I bought it, I had to change the exhaust system and see to a few details. The cost? A little over $1,000. Most drivers would ask themselves, "Why put $1,000 into a car that is worth less than $2,000?"

I saw it differently. If the $1,000 in repairs would buy me another year with it, I could put off a major expenditure for another few months, not to mention the fact that my car's cost per year of use would be lower. Any additional year spent with an end-of-life model is a year of financial reprieve. A more recent model would automatically be more expensive in taxes and insurance.

Plus, a paid-off car lets you set money aside for future expenses. **I never had to make monthly car payments: that was great.** You feel like someone else is paying for a future fleet of cars. Old-beater drivers thank those who buy new cars. Without them, we couldn't do what we do.

In the end, I sold that 1998 car for $860 in May 2016. It got me from point A to point B for five years, at a fraction of the price of a new car.

Recently, I carpooled with someone who was pretty well off. He drove a nice SUV. I have to admit, it was great. "I bought it used," he said. "It's a 2011. Anyway, in high-end cars, who can tell the difference between a 2011 and a 2015? The difference in terms of utility isn't worth the difference in price."

His comment pleasantly surprised me. Even though the guy was a millionaire, he understood that buying a new car for $50,000 was a needless luxury for him. **If you have $50,000 to put into a car, I hope you have maxed out your TFSA, your RRSP and your children's RESPs.**

Of celebrities and breakdowns

But then there is another myth: what if the car broke down? As if that would be the end of the world.

A new car, while more recent, is not immune to breakdowns or mechanical problems. But that's people's perception. Having a used car periodically maintained and inspected minimizes this sort of problem. Plus, a CAA membership is the old-car driver's best friend. It's insurance in case something goes wrong.

Even though rationally we know that for long-term financial health it's better to buy a used car than a new one, marketing is powerful. To sell cars, they hire funny, friendly or beautiful spokespeople.

They are not selling a product, but rather an image, as if a heap of metal in a different colour or with a different shape and logo could really have an impact on our social market value.

Car makers fight hard to push consumers beyond rationality. Getting a new car every four years is the ultimate in financial loss. We enjoy a fraction of the useful life of the car but pay the highest cost annually. Plus, car prices are so high that in ads, they prefer not to mention the actual price. What they sell is a monthly, semi-monthly or weekly payment—or simply a lifestyle.

In the CEGEP and university classes I teach, I've lost track of the number of discussions we have had about cars.

When students in administration complain that their budget is tight but they are driving this year's car, I have to rub their faces in the contradiction. At age eighteen or twenty, buying a new or late-model car significantly compromises financial security and the ability to invest. Like shoemakers who don't repair their own shoes, these administration students aren't putting into practice the principles they are learning.

FREE TIP!

One day, my cousin shared a great trick with me. Every time she feels the urge to buy a new vehicle, she has her car cleaned inside out to get it ready to sell. You know, the sort of "pimp my ride" treatment where they clean the car right down to the engine? When she leaves the garage, she ends up telling herself, "If it weren't already mine, I'd buy it." That's $30 well spent to make a more rational decision.

Financial lies

What about 0 percent or 0.9 percent financing? These sorts of deals are about as authentic as Santa Claus. Car companies are in debt themselves, so they are hardly going to finance their clients for free. So how can they offer such low rates of financing?

It's easy: they include the financing in the sale price of the car. And given that dealers don't offer discounts to clients who pay cash, people who pay cash are implicitly subsidizing buyers who take the financing. Basically, buy-now-pay-later purchases have become so common that dealers develop their business model around vehicle financing.

Maybe you have recently experienced the moment when the salesperson tells you he has "low margins" on the car sold. The ultimate insult is when they claim to be selling at the wholesale price.

No matter what documents they show you, salespeople are lying. At the end of the year, they receive a commission for the number of vehicles sold. Selling new cars is profitable, and the buyer isn't getting the better part of the deal. Period.

And what about the implicit costs that are never considered when calculating the pros and cons of a car? For example, all the money tied up in building, maintaining and heating a garage, the primary purpose of which is to provide shelter for cars. In suburban paradise, it's incredible to see the importance placed on the personal car; double garages, oversized entrances and the weekly washing of cars are proof of our car-centrism.

Of course, we all need to use a car from time to time. But we should think about the importance placed on them in the family budget. Can we question the need to own one? Can we stop thinking that cars reflect our personality? A sporty, luxury SUV can be driven by people who are anything but adventurous or athletic. A luxury car can be driven by someone in debt up to their eyeballs. A bus rider can be a millionaire or someone on social assistance.

A car impresses envious onlookers for a few minutes.

But does driving a nice car make us freer, more powerful or healthier? Are we more attractive, competent or charismatic?

Does a Jaguar mean boomers don't need Viagra? Does it prevent stressed-out professionals from getting depressed or confer coolness upon the nerdy?

> We are victims of our desires. We are our own financial hangman. You need to ask yourself the following question: do you really need a new car, beyond the basic functions? And we can go one step further: do you really need a car at all?

A CAR
DO YOU REALLY NEED IT?

L et's go one step beyond the question of buying a new car. We can examine the need to own a car at all.

Every dollar spent on a car carries an opportunity cost. For instance, reconsidering the monthly car budget might allow people to put more into savings or vacation. **The truth is, often people can't find room in the budget to save for their children's education, but they can find it to add options to a car.** Why not just work less to strike a better balance? Would a dollar you don't spend in your car budget let you take advantage of life and enjoy new activities? It's not a popular way to think: in Quebec, 451,354 new cars were sold in 2015, an increase of 5.7 percent over the previous year.[1]

Unfortunately, most of our cities have been developed around the needs of the automobile, so it would be utopian to imagine a world without personal cars. But for those of us who live in urban environments, we should be taking another look at the number of cars we think we need. With bike sharing, car sharing and the

---

1   http://www.statcan.gc.ca/tables-tableaux/sum-som/l01/cst01/trade36e-eng.htm

revolution in the taxi industry, we ignore thinking about how we use transportation at our own peril.

A technology revolution

When Uber first came onto the scene, objections arose based on taxation and protectionism, but these obscured a greater reality: solutions are out there that limit the need to own a personal car.

In Quebec, for example, the creation of Téo Taxi and the cavalier arrival of Uber transformed the taxi experience in Montreal, offering new possibilities:

- ✔ ordering taxis using a smartphone;
- ✔ travelling by electric car;
- ✔ free wi-fi in vehicles; and
- ✔ mobile payment.

We've been invited to join the technology revolution, but we are still left with the traditional idea of the taxi. We have not yet advanced to the concept of shared taxis, which Uber offers in other cities through UberPOOL, allowing customers to share a trip with strangers picked up along the way.

Car sharing also means cost sharing. Operational research into transportation has made it possible to optimize public transit and make private transportation sharing easier. Basically, complex mathematical calculations are enabling this evolution in technology. Using a shared service allows the sharing of the development costs.

A different method of transportation for each stage of life
I have gone through periods in my life when I used public transit, bikes, cars, car sharing, and so on. Your needs vary depending on your circumstances.

For example, since I work partly outside Montreal and my children go to daycare far from home, using my personal car is convenient. Like many people, I have developed the reflex of getting behind the wheel for pretty much anything. But once my children are old enough to go to school, and the days of strollers and diaper bags are behind me, I will be able to walk more and use public transit more easily.

One thing is certain: in urban areas, if it's the norm for every person to own a car, there are questions we need to ask ourselves.

My sister and her spouse, who are both in their forties, have never owned a car. They don't have kids, but they are nonetheless the exception to the rule: two carless professionals are practically extraterrestrials. And yet, not having a car gives them tremendous financial leeway. Their house is paid for, their RRSPs and TFSAs runneth over, and they travel more. That sounds like freedom to me.

To justify having a personal car, the total cost of taxi-run errands, public transit passes, and charges for rental cars needs to rival the cost of that purchase. Very few people do the math. People want freedom. But a car requires time, management and maintenance. It can also eliminate a sizable chunk of your financial freedom.

Energy and financial inefficiency
We also need to consider the weight of vehicles, which has changed over the years. From the 1970s to the mid-1980s, the

average weight of a vehicle dropped dramatically.[1] Then, for around twenty years, it increased, and it has now more or less stabilized. When you think about it, it is pretty crazy to move more than 2,000 kilograms over hundreds of kilometres to transport an 80-kilogram person.

Clearly, personal cars make no sense in terms of energy consumption. If we were to count all the empty seats in the cars on the road every day, we might be surprised at their inefficiency.

Now, with the benefit of apps, sharing rides with people in your neighbourhood just makes sense. It's 7:30 a.m. and I'm in the suburb of Repentigny; there must be thousands of people heading to Montreal. It's time for technology to help us get in touch with one another and share time and resources.

I am by no means anti-car. I just want us to think about the place of the car in society, and to look at it through a financial lens.

We mistakenly believe that taking public transit is a question of wealth. But just because you have enough money to buy a car doesn't mean that you should. Public transit isn't reserved for the poor; it's merely a different way of getting around.

A few years ago, I didn't own a vehicle. One day, as my brother-in-law and I were waiting in line at the corner store, a woman said, "Anyway, I want my next boyfriend to be rich. I don't want to go out with a guy who doesn't have a car." There you have it. According to that woman, someone like me was poor. She equated owning a car with social status.

Everything is a question of perception. Redefining concepts can help us see more clearly. For example, if you say you own

---

1   http://www.nrcan.gc.ca/energy/efficiency/transportation/cars-light-trucks/buying/16755

this year's model of sports car, you might be perceived as someone who has worked a good chunk of his life to buy a rolling heap of metal that goes fast. Cynical? Perhaps, but it's the truth.

Question every new purchase

So why should owning a car be an obvious choice? Because the car you have now is ready for the scrapyard? Before shopping for another, you could look at your present situation and ask yourself: do I really need it? Life changes. Yesterday's yes could be tomorrow's no.

When you have a regular job at a single location, planning travel is easier. In my own case, with young children and a number of jobs, it's hard to manage getting around without a car. But once my kids are more independent, why would I own a car when we live two minutes from a bus stop, less than seven minutes from a metro station, and a hand wave from hopping in a taxi?

Even those who live in the country or the suburbs should ask themselves whether they have made the best geographical choice. With cities developing suburbs like it's the twentieth century, it's hard not to become a victim of urban development. But we have all helped maintain and support this type of development, the traces of which will remain for years to come.

Suburbs lack density, and stores tend to be located outside residential neighbourhoods. The result is urban sprawl and difficulty developing public transit. Why leave city centres? Why do we fuel this fantasy of being alone together? All of these life choices make a future without a car (or at least with fewer cars) impossible. Transportation needs to be part and parcel of our thinking, just like proximity to services and schools.

Do you really need a car?

The answer is yes for many, and I'm not casting stones. There is currently one car per adult at my house. But I still aspire to be a car-free household.

Is that something you can imagine? If not, I understand. But can you imagine eliminating one or two from your driveway?

Everyone has their own road, their own efforts and their own reality . . .

BALANCE
DO YOU REALLY NEED IT?

The balance we spend so much time seeking may be one of the most hackneyed concepts in what I call the business of well-being.

The reality is that everyone lives in constant disequilibrium, and that disequilibrium has played a part in all of the world's major successes. There is a cost to a lack of balance. It has an impact on our personal finances; it can pay off by generating revenue, but it also creates a lot of extra expenses. Welcome to the world of imbalance.

Accepting imbalances

As you strive to build your life, prove your worth and get ahead at work or with your savings, sometimes you can find yourself out of balance. Actually, we don't just find ourselves there—it hits. Without warning.

We may think we are better or stronger than others. We tell ourselves we can take it. Other people are lazy. Other people are weak. That isn't necessarily the case, though we may want to believe it. There are only twenty-four hours in a day. How

long can we burn the candle at both ends? What are
the consequences of our choices? Will mind and
body follow?

One day, as part of a presentation to students at the CEGEP
Régional de Lanaudière in L'Assomption, I interviewed an
executive who belonged to an organization that promoted wom-
en's career advancement. During our discussion, she said, "I've
learned to accept a certain lack of balance."

It's reassuring when someone acknowledges imbalance and
speaks openly about it. Like brothers- and sisters-in-arms in self-
inflicted discomfort, it makes you feel as though you have a
common mission.

In some respects, imbalance leads to great things and great
accomplishments, like when you prepare day and night for an
exam or a sports competition. But it also takes away from other
things; for example, working too much can take a toll on your
family life.

I am one of the most unbalanced people I know (as regards
my life, not my mind, thankfully). It sounds strange to say, and I
don't know who I'm trying to prove something to, but I definitely
revel in a constant lack of balance.

It all started when I was working and going to school at the
same time. I gave up sports, regular sleep and leisure to concentrate on those two aspects of my life. It was sort of a semi-
conscious act of faith in building a career.

That was the point when I started burning the candle at both
ends. **I had to study to be better than other students. I had to
work to become financially secure. Duty came first.** My mantra
was, "I may not be the smartest, but I am going to work the
hardest."

With a zombie-like single-mindedness, I was able to ignore my own needs for a long stretch of my life. I was a machine. An imperfect machine that was able to forgo happiness to survive in a cruel world. But I couldn't pull off such a feat today. Why? Because that pace couldn't be maintained. And, most importantly, it resulted in self-destructive thoughts and behaviour, brought on by the frustrations created by imbalance.

Work

You have to deliver more than others to be professionally recognized. You have to perform better. You have to outdo others and yourself. You don't create value without effort.

When you look at people you admire, you often see the tip of the iceberg but not the base: long hours developing skills, honing their craft, going where others won't and sacrificing parts of their personal lives.

But all of this has consequences. When the imbalance phase drags on too long, it can create a sense that something's missing, leaving the impression that part of your life is lacking or that you are driving too fast. While others are quietly taking a break at the side of the road, you tear down the hill so fast that you can't even tell what direction you're headed in.

Excess

Sometimes you have to veer into excess to become aware of your imbalance. The type of excess varies from person to person: overspending, an overly strict diet, overwork, studying too much, overeating, drinking too much, doing drugs, engaging in too much sex, spending too much time on the Internet or hitting the gym too often. Excess ends up interfering with your ability to see clearly, to do what you need to do, in other words to **respect your values and goals.** Excess comes to the rescue as temporary compensation for depression, which can be caused by imbalance. The wheel keeps turning.

We plunge into excess voluntarily, telling ourselves we will make up for it later. We tell ourselves that we will be able to get our head above water in a few weeks, then in a few months, which ends up turning into a few years. We can blow through our forties without any moments of calm, all because of a self-imposed relentless pace.

No one forces us to push ourselves this way, but desire generates ambition, and ambition generates the habits needed to fulfill it. We wind up wearing blinders, ones we put on ourselves.

As a result, we can't see or understand what is around us, ignoring what is plainly obvious to others.

A classic example

Let's take Paul. Paul works hard to carve out his place in the world. He is finishing school. He is athletic, young, rebellious and a decent guy. One of the largest accounting firms in the world has just recruited him.

For Paul, snagging this position is the culmination of hard years living at subsistence levels. He starts his job, and to prove himself, he works too much, somewhat grudgingly. Inventory is managed using the FIFO method, which stands for "first in, first out." Coincidentally, there's also a FIFO that applies to employees: fit in or fuck off.

In this example, I could have replaced "accountant" with engineer, lawyer or any other job that demands discipline and professional volunteer work. Basically, any job with an annual salary.

Every extra hour you put in is proof of your commit-ment to the company. But the reality is that it's mainly about profitability for the partners or shareholders.

To maintain this level of commitment, some people are offered carrots: one day, they could find themselves at the top of the pyramid of retained earnings. That's the carrot that keeps Paul at work. And he works hard. More and more. He puts in hours like never before. Six or seven days a week.

To look good, he doesn't even account for all his hours on the time sheet that requires an entry every six minutes (a tenth of an hour). Long live billable hours. Paul doesn't really have time for anything else. Lunch hour is relegated to the sidelines. He gobbles down a sandwich in front of his computer, having had no time to plan his groceries for the week. Soon he stops going home for dinner.

The more active Paul is at work, the more sedentary he becomes. His waistline gradually expands. "It's because I'm get-ting older," he tells himself. He never unwinds. His wife com-plains he's always at work. He tells himself he's working to make their lives better.

Paul is starting to feel bad, mentally and physically. His rela-tionship gradually shifts from convivial to conflictual. To avoid unpleasantness, Paul doesn't go home, because it could stop him from functioning. I mean, it's bad enough at work.

Children arrive in the midst of this madness. Family pres-sures start to build. Paul thinks he is stronger than other people, but he winds up ignoring his needs. Since he no longer eats at home, he goes out more and spends more time on leisure activi-ties to make up for what he's missing. He distracts himself by buying things.

Paul buys the latest tech gadget, which doesn't bring him the happiness he thought it would. Finally, having to engage in outsourcing because of overwork brings him back to square one: he is not really any richer.

In fact, he is living larger, but with less time and capacity to make the most of it. It's all an illusion. Then his marriage breaks down because of his mistakes, his lack of time and the stress of the constant arguments. The wounds run deep. His heart is broken, and cynicism sets in. Love is dead, and so is his heart.

At this point, Paul understands the price of having lost his way. His financial health is seriously suffering when the time comes to divide the assets and pay alimony. Excess catches up with him at the bend in the road. It stares him in the face: he suddenly realizes he hasn't measured up to his expectations.

He becomes a pale imitation of a cardboard soap opera character. Failure caused by imbalance stings. Starting from good intentions—to make his life better—Paul fell into a series of corrosive behaviours that gradually ate away at his soul.

The vicious circle of imbalance

Like a bridge that reaches mechanical resonance and then collapses,[1] imbalances (professional, financial, dietary, what have you) can create a chain reaction, leaving you wondering which imbalance started it all.

The order in which these imbalances appear varies from person to person, but the underlying principle is the same: **an imbalance of any sort can have a serious impact on personal finances.**

---

1   www.youtube.com/watch?v=uhWQ5zr5_xc

Should we recognize and accept our imbalances, or gradually sink into them? It's hard to know when we don't have time to ask ourselves the question. Things keep moving. Everything is fast and running on autopilot.

- ✔ You don't make love; you get laid.
- ✔ You don't eat; you stuff your face.
- ✔ You don't have a drink; you get wasted.
- ✔ Excess leads to excess.

Of course, it's not always a catastrophic scenario. Sometimes there are nuances: rather than succumbing, we simply learn to live with disappointments and disillusionment. We make do with a false sense of satiety. One day we find ourselves in a life that has no flavour or smell.

So how do we achieve balance? What is the golden mean? This equilibrium is highly personal, and you need to bump up against imbalance to find it. At least, that's what I think.

A love-hate relationship with balance

Even as we try to achieve balance, we also run away from it. On the one hand, we know that, without imbalance, we might not have pushed ourselves to achieve certain objectives or realize certain dreams. On the other hand, imbalance has consequences we want to avoid. So we try to walk the tightrope of imbalance. As we walk the high wire, we think we are in control of our movements. But all it takes is a gust of wind for disaster to strike.

What drives people to excess, always wanting to feel the intoxication of the unknown and pursue the next new thing? Clearly, we aspire to something else. Something else that is constantly new. We are condemned to want what we don't have.

Personal finances at the centre of balance

All of this brings me back to the concept of leeway (see "Financial Leeway: Do You Really Need It?" on page 1). Without a certain degree of balance, personal finances end up factoring into all this. Balance is necessary, even when you try to avoid it.

Our ability to make money and fund our dreams depends on our ability to stay within the acceptable limits of imbalance. How do you know if you've stepped over the line? How far can you stretch yourself before you break?

When it comes to managing personal finances, few people take a holistic approach, where the numbers don't do all the talking. Balance is that nirvana that is always off in the distance; the minute we feel as if we're getting close to it, it shoots off ahead of us again.

We have an unhealthy tendency to be dissatisfied, to feel something is missing even when we don't know what it is. So we throw ourselves into an endless quest for balance. Do you really need balance? I still dream of achieving it.

MARRIAGE
DO YOU REALLY NEED IT?

My parents were married on August 3, 1968, in a post-religious Quebec, in which, to be socially accepted, you still had to get married to have sex, have children and live out your days with a modicum of happiness. Times have well and truly changed in the ensuing decades. So why do we need to get married today?

According to the Institut de la statistique du Québec (ISQ), almost two-thirds of births in Quebec occur outside wedlock.[1] Still according to the ISQ, in 2008 there were 22,053 marriages and 13,899 divorces. Clearly, we are a long way from the magical thinking of "till death do us part."

Why make a promise that, statistically, more than half of all couples will break? In the referendum of life, it's the option that wouldn't win. The opposition party would challenge the validity of the vote, and a new conjugal election would have to be held.

We could change the usual marriage vows to "I promise to love, honour and cherish you until . . .

---

1   http://www.stat.gouv.qc.ca/quebec-chiffre-main/pdf/qcm2015_an.pdf

I change my mind." It wouldn't be as romantic, but it would be more realistic.

Of course, back when people had a life expectancy of thirty years, it was easier to keep a promise of longevity in marriage.

When cynicism sets in

Financially speaking, there is good reason to be cynical about marriage. Why? First, because for many people their wedding day means renewing their mortgage for twenty-five years. To justify the expense of a wedding at a critical point in our financial lives, we invoke feelings, appearances, and a false association between love and money.

Start with the engagement ring, which is supposed to cost the prospective groom three months' salary. Excuse me? Why spend thousands of dollars for a piece of rock that gives no more pleasure and has no more use than fashion jewellery bought at Ardène? What many see as the race for the ring is superficial and has no real bearing on love. "How many carats is the diamond—one or two? What? Not even one carat? Are you sure about this guy?"

Let's face it: **a ring is a symbol, not an investment in real estate, or a stay at a five-star hotel.** What actually distinguishes a diamond from cubic zirconia?

After the ring comes the dress, which is the most expensive piece of clothing a person ever buys and the one worn the least amount of time. It will hang in a walk-in closet for years, nostalgic testimony to a time when the couple didn't hate each other so much.

Then there is all the marketing around weddings. There is a term for it: the "wedding tax." Wedding photographers cost more than studio photographers. They will spend the day taking pictures of staged moments to create false memories. And don't forget the souvenir video, with the arranged scenes shot at least twice. The wedding tax applies to everything: the reception hall, the limousine service, the event planning, the menu, and on and on.

Whether you're talking about a $10,000, $20,000, $50,000 or $100,000 wedding, it's always the same thing. Everyone endures a celebration where the only people who aren't counting the minutes until it's over are up in the front. The guests are hot and restless and can't wait until they can talk to their friends and have a drink. But first, there is the endless receiving line to congratulate the newlyweds. And, of course, you must tell the bride just how beautiful she looks, otherwise she will feel that her manicure, pedicure, hairstylist, makeup artist, dress, and shoes she is teetering on were all money down the drain.

The party finally gets started: cocktails, dinner, cutlery clinking on glasses, a little emceeing by a wannabe performer, the throwing of the bouquet, dancing, booze, and good-night-it's-time-to-go-home. Obviously, "YMCA" will play at some point in the proceedings.

The next day, the debit is entered on the balance sheet, and the happy couple is no better off than the night before. They just threw an absurdly big party that could have paid for 200 or 300 dinners with friends at home, or two or three trips!

But no matter, they're married. Love isn't about money, you may say.

Well, no, but is it worth the price? Is it worth not having a down payment for a house? Does it justify having to take a car loan rather than paying for the car in cash? Is it worth neglecting your retirement savings and scaling back your kids' registered education savings plan? Because nothing is free. Every choice has consequences. It's called opportunity cost: every dollar spent on one budget line item prevents us from allocating that dollar to another budget line item.

No problem, you say. The guests give us gifts, which offset some of the expenses. It may even cover the cost of the wedding! Oh, so **you shamelessly got your parents, friends and family to subsidize your party?**

An invitation . . . to spend

I'm not trying to burst the bubble of the future happy couple who choose this sort of wedding, but rather to look reality in the eye.

This is the reaction of your lucky friends who get an invitation to your wedding:

"Honey . . ."

"Yes?"

"We got another save-the-date."

"Oh no! Not another one! We're already going to two weddings this summer."

"It's August 6."

"You've got to be kidding me. In the middle of my vacation!"

"Yeah, I'm going to need two dresses. I can't wear the same thing twice with the same group of friends. I'm going to need a purse too, maybe a new necklace and—"

"Good lord!"

Your invitation has just imposed an activity on your friends during their summer holidays, when they work like crazy all year to balance the budget and take care of their relationship. Plus, they will have to spend money on outfits, getting to the wedding and a babysitter for the kids.

Then your wife is asked to be maid of honour. She gets to wear a pastel dress that makes the bride's friends look like icing on a cake. Yet another dress that will be worn once because, outside the context of a wedding, it's not exactly attractive (admittedly, taste is subjective). Plus, there has to be a rehearsal to make sure the wedding doesn't flop. And here I was thinking marriages got screwed up after the ceremony and not during.

Then comes the fateful moment when you slip the cheque into an envelope. How much is it for a wedding gift these days? This is when you try to determine how big the wedding will be and how close you are to the future couple to come up with a gift that covers at least the cost of the invitation. The cheque means $300 less in the family vacation budget.

In the end, guests will have to spend hundreds of dollars for a party that doesn't give them the pleasure they would have had somewhere else for the same money. And we've only discussed the wedding itself! Often there is the bachelor party (which means karting, heavy drinking, a nightclub and a strip club) and bachelorette party (a day at the spa, dinner, cocktails and a nightclub), or perhaps a bridal shower, or a stag-and-doe. Basically, it's never-ending: **getting married means forcing your loved ones to whip out their chequebooks.**

And what about the future couple who like things exotic? On the invitation to the sunshine destination, they say, "No gifts. Just pay for your trip." Not to mention the princess with Snow White fantasies who wants to get married at Walt Disney World. It's your choice: either you decline the invitation or you don't make an annual contribution to your RRSP. As French chemist Antoine Lavoisier said, "Nothing is lost, nothing is created, everything is transformed."

The marriage you really need

Marriage has its uses, though: it gives spouses protection in case of death or separation. The legal act is based on signing papers, whether or not the ceremony is religious.

Why protect yourself? Because marriage creates automatic mechanisms in the event of a problem. For example, if the husband were to leave the wife for a woman their daughter's age, the separation of family assets would be done with more objectivity than if it were to occur amidst a barrage of insults and a war between lawyers.

The marriage contract is also particularly important when one of the spouses earns less than the other and spends more time taking care of the children. When common-law spouses separate, there is no value attributed to either of them, and everything has to be hashed out. That's why it's best to have a plan in place for protecting the vulnerable spouse.

How much do marriage documents cost? Not much. For a few hundred dollars you can get married in the afternoon without the pomp or circumstance. At the same time, you can make your will and living will, and, just like that, your family's future is settled for the time being, and everyone is protected by default under the marriage contract.

Before getting married, it's also a good idea to find out about the legal consequences of doing so, which don't figure into the lovefest pictures on Facebook.

So, what you really need is:

- ✔ a will;
- ✔ a living will; and
- ✔ financial planning (insurance, investments, etc.) for the surviving spouse.

FREE TIPS!

- Turn down invitations to weddings of people who aren't an extremely important part of your life.
- Don't worry—the couple won't be angry. After all, they may have sent you the invitation just to be polite!

So, do you really need to get married? You want to celebrate your love. Why not invite your family and friends to the courthouse and celebrate the contract you've signed? If you end up getting divorced, at least the party will have been cheaper, right?

But you don't need a $30,000 party.

SAVING
DO YOU REALLY NEED TO?

The problem with saving? Let's talk instead about the problem with not saving. The consequences aren't visible, immediate or certain. It's a bit like the sixteen-year-old boy who takes up smoking: he can't see his teeth at forty, his aged skin, his cancer-ridden lungs, his addiction, his coronary bypass or his inability to get it up. He certainly doesn't sense other people's discomfort with how he smells.

Not saving is like starting to smoke: at the beginning you enjoy it, you get into the habit, it becomes an addiction, and it's only later that you have to live with the negative consequences. Neglecting to save means denying your children opportunities when they are older or paying interest on stress-inducing debt you shouldn't have.

On the other hand, **saving gives you the freedom to walk away from it all, to change your life, to leave behind what you no longer need.** It's not about doing it, but about being able to do it. It frees the mind, destroying the glass cage that we sometimes feel we've built for ourselves. The one that's airtight and ends up suffocating us.

Who can tell at age twenty that they will be comfortable and happy with their lifestyle until the end of their days? Who can predict a separation, a critical illness, an accident, a head trauma or sudden depression? No one. No one is immune. So savings, in the form of a registered retirement savings plan (RRSP) or a tax-free savings account (TFSA), are also insur- ance against living on the street, collecting empties and sleeping in a shelter.

I know, you have to live your life. I get it. I'm not talking about becoming an ant. La Fontaine's fable about the carefree cricket and the diligent ant is probably one of life's greatest lessons. But somewhere between the cricket and the ant, there is the crick-ant: it sings 30 percent of the time and works 70 percent of the remaining business days. This is what you should try to aim for: save a set percentage of your salary systematically, the same way you eat regular meals or sit on the throne daily.

There's nothing wrong with spending money and having a life. I'm not saying you should become a fanatic, but there is not much point in flooring it when you are fifty metres away from a brick wall.

In a world where we are told we must be truly unhappy if we don't spend enough, you have to exercise a bit of temporal resis-tance: deferring gratification or enduring the pain of not spend-ing. Not spending feels like you're depriving yourself in the short term, which can make you unhappy. But exercising restraint will actually result in short-, medium- and long-term happiness.

Don't leave money on the table
RRSPs and TFSAs, despite their simplicity, are sometimes misun-derstood. They are registered investments, which means you can

invest in different types of vehicles and register them in an RRSP or TFSA. For example, you can invest in stocks, bonds, guaranteed investment certificates, mutual fund shares or even cash.

Why associate savings with these two tax vehicles? Because they make it possible to avoid paying tax on certain types of returns or to postpone paying taxes. When governments offer a tax benefit like this and you don't take advantage of it, you're leaving money on the table. Honestly, leaving free money on the table is like going to the bank machine, entering your PIN, seeing $200 come out, and walking away without taking the cash.[1] **Not contributing to an RRSP or TFSA is giving your money to the next person in line.**

Speaking of money down the drain, when employees decide not to contribute the maximum to a pension plan (or a group RRSP) with an employer contribution, they are also leaving money on the table by giving up the employer contribution. It's like saying, "Thanks, boss, but I don't want part of my salary." You have to be rich not to take advantage of a benefit. Or else you don't have the means to save.

Ironically, not saving is a selfish act: not having money when you retire determines the assistance you will need from society. People who don't save count on a better pension from Old Age Security and will pay little or no tax. One could argue that not saving is premeditated theft from others. Therefore, saving is a personal choice with societal consequences.

---

1   Not contributing to a tax-free savings account means not taking advantage of a tax-free return on your investment. For example, if you invest $1,000 in a TFSA in stocks and you get a return of $100, you won't be taxed on that money. Not using a TFSA is giving up a tax benefit.

Is it possible to contribute the maximum to a TFSA and an RRSP? Yes, for people who are very comfortable financially. The average person who earns between $40,000 and $60,000 per year can still make a significant contribution. Then it's a matter of choice. Personally, I've committed to consistently contributing the maximum to an RRSP every year. Is it easy? No.

Some years, like the year a child is born or the year you buy a house, are like a millstone on your budget. But every time I hear someone with an annual salary of $40,000 or $50,000 say, "I don't have enough to save," I'm dubious. How can they say that? Plenty of people live on much less.

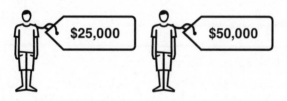

If we compare someone who earns $25,000 a year with someone who earns $50,000 a year, it's possible neither has savings. However, the individual who earns $50,000 can't look the other one in the eye and say, "I don't have enough to save." That person may be living beyond their means, but they can't earn twice the gross salary of the other person and not take a good, hard look at themselves.

And where does the TFSA fit into all of this? I used one to help save the down payment for a duplex when I was thirty. Since that time, I haven't contributed to one, but that's a matter of choice. I'll start again soon.

Investing can mean real estate too. Or you can decide to invest in a private business. It's all a question of distribution of risk and your personal situation. **The message you should come away with is that you have to invest—and invest in yourself— as early as possible, no matter what form that takes.**

When we talk about saving, there is always someone who will say, as on a dating site: "I'm a foodie. I love great restaurants, films and travelling. Basically, I love to live in the moment!" Hello! Who doesn't? Who doesn't like their taste buds to cry out in pleasure and their mouth to water? Who doesn't like being on a beach sipping a cold cocktail? Could you try to be a little more original? It's the sort of thing that could be translated as, "I deserve more than others, because they will settle for much less." Everyone wants the good life. Isn't a foodie just the cricket from the La Fontaine fable?

The other view of saving

As a society, we are stuck on the idea that RRSPs and TFSAs are strictly for retirement savings. That needs to change. Contributing annually to them means giving yourself the opportunity to take a nice trip at age thirty, to buy a house, or to stop working because you want to. For me, it means freedom. Tomorrow's freedom that I'm putting away for today. Like a squirrel getting ready for winter.

How much do you have to save? One thing is certain: you have to start saving before you start a family, because otherwise it will be a shock to your system. Yes, fine, but how much money do you have to put aside by age thirty-five? I always give the same answer, relatively speaking, and I always get tomatoes thrown at me.

Obviously, we're talking here about a rule of thumb for people who are earning above the minimum wage. Let's quantify it using an average salary. And since it's good for the prostate, I will go out on a limb and say, based on empirical rules, that **you need to aim for net assets equal to about two years of gross salary.**

So, for an annual salary of $50,000 at age thirty-five, you should have saved at least $100,000 in net assets in different forms: capital in your house, capital in real estate, RRSPs, TFSAs, non-registered investments in the stock market, an investment in a private company, and so on.

If, after finishing school, you systematically put 18 percent of your gross income into an RRSP, you will have handily saved in excess of the amount equal to two years' gross salary by the time you reach thirty-five (unless, obviously, your salary skyrocketed between age thirty-four and thirty-five). Other approaches are possible, but for the average person who doesn't experience an extraordinary windfall, it's a rule of thumb.

Obviously, reading this, many people will say, "Yes, but in *my* case . . . blah blah blah . . ." You're right. I'm not talking about people who have lost a lot of money through bad luck in business, people who had cancer at age twenty-three, or people who had six kids with three different spouses between age twenty and twenty-six.

When you invest in an RRSP, you can deduct your contribution and get a tax refund, but you pay the tax if you withdraw the amount you invest. As for a TFSA, you contribute with after-tax dollars (there is no deduction or refund when you contribute), and the returns are tax sheltered.

So, if I'm willing to speculate with my savings, TFSAs are interesting because they potentially multiply income with no tax impact when I withdraw money. For example, if I invest $1,000 in a TFSA and the investment is worth $10,000 in three years, the $9,000 gain won't be taxable. Isn't that great?

But everyone has their own strategy. None is perfect. You just need to choose the one that suits your economic situation based on your choices and financial obligations.

If you're reading this book, you've finished school, and you haven't consulted anyone to develop a savings plan, this may be the push you need to take the first step. Does it make sense to spend months planning for vacations, fishing trips, children and marriage, but ignore managing your financial security?

Take charge of your financial life

Your goal with savings is not to retire in Florida, turning your skin to leather. What you are trying to do is build a fund that will allow you to say, "I'm doing it," "I quit," "Go fuck yourself," "Pack your bags; we're leaving for Paris," or "*Carpe diem!*" a few years down the line. **Saving gives you choices**.

That said, you need to ensure you understand the front-line banking system. In the branch, mutual fund representatives have to feed the machine. Their main goal is to offer advice, but they also have to hit their targets. Every year, they need to sell a certain amount in mortgages, investments, credit cards, lines of credit, or insurance on different types of credit. Don't hate them: they're just doing their jobs.

To those who say, "There's no point in saving with returns so low," I would answer that future needs don't change. So you have to save more when returns are lower. That way, if the market picks up, you get a return on a larger amount, which will make up for the lean years.

Knowing this, why doesn't the average person save more? There are parallels with diet. **Saving means setting a budget**

and limiting bad spending decisions. The same way a diet means making a calorie budget and avoiding food that has too many empty calories.

But people are tempted by bad spending decisions just as they are tempted to eat a Big Mac. Plenty of people are in dire financial straits, and plenty of people are overweight. Yet many of them were balanced both financially and physically when they were eighteen. What's the advantage of a healthy diet? Excess ends up showing in the mirror, and we can react. Otherwise, someone might end up telling us, "Put on a little weight there, I see!" But when you don't save and are in debt, there is no one to remind you of it regularly. You tuck your bank statements in a drawer and live in denial. You won't often hear, "Put on a little debt there, I see. Looks like around $10,000!"

As with your diet, saving requires ongoing, daily control. Little efforts and daily choices end up making a big difference over the years. Having the equivalent of two years' salary set aside by age thirty-five is like having flat abs at the same age. We think people who have them are lucky but don't admit that we could be "lucky" too if we made different choices.

So, saving: do you really need to? The answer is, do you have the means not to?

There's no point in telling me, "Yes, but my friend died at thirty in an accident. He couldn't take his money with him." True. You're right. But what would he have done if he hadn't died in a tragic accident? Who's to say, but he would have known that, statistically, he was likely to die an old man.

A GOOD CREDIT SCORE
DO YOU REALLY NEED IT?

Talking to young adults about the importance of their credit score is like talking to a party full of diabetics about Coca-Cola Classic: it's not the target audience. But it should be. The value of a good credit score is underappreciated.

In an increasingly impersonal world, saying, "He's a nice kid. He's the son of What's His Name over on Dion Street," doesn't cut it. Credit scores are like blood tests for consumer behaviour: there's no bias, and a stranger can assess them.

A credit history details our relationship with credit, financing and loans. The score is our overall grade for credit.

One day, while I was studying at HEC Montréal, we had a substitute lecturer, whose name I won't mention. The guy wasn't terribly interested in talking about assets or revenue (even though the course was called Assets and Revenue). As lecturers go, he was bad. Truly bad. But he absolutely wanted to talk to us about credit.

He emphasized one thing: **in today's world, without a good credit score, you're nothing.** Was he speaking personally? Was he alluding to his own shortcomings? No matter. That day, he did what he set out to do, because that's when I started to get interested in the mechanisms of the credit history and score.

Don't judge a book by its cover

When you go into a bank, you can be as sexy as Brad Pitt in *Thelma & Louise*, wear Leonardo DiCaprio's suit from *The Wolf of Wall Street* or show cleavage down to your navel, but your branch representative is interested in other things. Banks generally look at a few criteria, including:

- ✔ your ability to pay (income, debt, lifestyle, etc.);
- ✔ collateral (or co-signers); and
- ✔ your credit score.

Broadly speaking, you can group these three things, and they form the pillar of access to credit. People are aware of their income and the collateral they can offer. But the value of their credit behaviour is another story.

Who cares about your credit history?

Whether it's the bank that admires your spunk as you make your loan application or your prospective landlord who is worried about not being paid, there are many good reasons for others to want access to your credit history.

Say it's spring and you want to buy a new car. Your dealer doesn't have any objection, but before financing the car, he wants to know your credit score. Are you an unreliable bender of the truth or someone who's organized and diligent? Your credit history includes personal information, credit information (credit cards, lines of credit, etc.), banking information (accounts, bounced cheques), public information (e.g., bankruptcy) and more.

How do credit scores work?

Generally speaking, credit scores vary between 300 and 900. For excellent credit, your score needs to be 760 or more. The data is compiled by credit bureaus. In Canada, the two main bureaus are Equifax and TransUnion. The two companies' clients (for example, banks) pay for the information they require.

In theory, your authorization is needed for someone to access your credit history. Obviously, since such a request is generally tied to an application for credit, you would rarely refuse it.

How to wreck or improve your credit score

When you access your credit history, you may be disappointed by your score. It's like the moment you realize the love-of-your-life-of-the-day doesn't share your feelings. How can my score be so low? Why? Why is my score lower than my brother's or my less affluent friend's?

Don't panic: there are things you can do to improve it. We can't be sure how the score is calculated or the effect of good or bad behaviour on it. It's a closely guarded secret. But we do know that the calculation is based on five main factors.[1]

1. Payment history

If you regularly miss the payment deadline for any balances owing, it could hurt your credit score. And if you've ever received

---

1   https://www.canada.ca/en/services/finance/debt.html

a threatening phone call from a collection agent, your score could be affected.

2. Reasonable use of available credit

Are you the type to carry a balance of $2,000 on your credit card with a limit of $2,500? You should know that your use of credit should generally be limited to 35 percent of all available credit.

3. Period covered by your credit history

Do you change credit cards with the direction of the wind? Remember that it's better to have a long credit history with your accounts. If you have had a platonic relationship with a credit card for the past ten years, you have a longer history than a friend who changes credit cards to get an annual $20 gift. Why not hang on to the oldest accounts? It's a sign of stability.

4. Number of requests for information

Every time you use buy-now-pay-later plans, that's another credit check. Likewise, if you go to a sporting event and you're offered a beach towel for applying for a credit card, you are sending the signal that you need more credit.

When you apply for credit, you need to ask yourself whether you really need it. You also have to ask yourself other important questions like, do I really need another beach towel or baseball cap?

5. Credit versatility

Some people don't like using several types of credit—but it's actually a way you can improve your credit score. If you have a credit card, it's a good idea to have a line of credit too, even if you rarely use it.

You'll notice that these points are contradictory at some level. Overall, I'm suggesting that it's best to have several sources of credit but to limit the number of applications. The important thing with credit is to act rationally.

A basic principle remains: pay your balance when it's due. With minimum payments, some people pump up their debt with enough helium that it achieves liftoff and escapes their grasp.

Credit scores and love

I can hear you protesting, "I'm not exactly going to ask my next Tinder date for a credit score!" Obviously not. But the financial habits of a romantic partner have a direct impact on a couple's financial life.

When you want to rent an apartment and your partner's credit score suggests they have an addiction to late payments, what do you do? Does this compromise your chances of finding an apartment? What about when you want to borrow to buy a condo: will you have access to credit?

FREE TIP!

The next time you apply for credit, such as to renew your mortgage or renegotiate your home equity line of credit, ask the banking representative for your score: he or she has it right there on the screen. It's simple, it doesn't cost you anything, and it's faster than with Equifax or TransUnion. Every time you renew your mortgage, take advantage of the opportunity to check that your score is improving.

Protecting your credit score opens up your world to possibility.

Do you weigh yourself regularly? Do you measure your waistline by checking whether you can wear a particular pair of pants?

You have to check your credit score too. Is it blemished? How would you know? It's imperative that you take an interest.

So, after reading this chapter, do you think you really need a good credit score?

BEING ABLE TO AFFORD IT
DO YOU REALLY NEED IT?

"**C**ome on, McSween, you can afford that, with the money you make!"

Every time someone says that to me, I always wonder what sort of simplistic analysis they must have done to reach that conclusion.

First of all, most of the time, **you can earn a good living without meeting short-, medium- and long-term obligations.** For example, you don't change the windows in your house every year, but you have to provide for this expense as if you were living in a condo.

Second, you can earn a lot of money but have more debts than assets.

Everyone lives with their own past and current realities. And they also live with a certain amount of uncertainty about the future.

Will I lose my job one day?	Will I stay mentally sharp?	Should I help my parents out?

123

Planning for the future rarely means just thinking about old age. For some people, "being able to afford it" means having cash in the bank. For others, it means having access to credit. For yet others, it means having a salary that covers disbursements (or cash withdrawals) today.

Finally, for some people, being able to afford it is purely theoretical. For these people, everything is a matter of perception and not a question of financial capacity. They will carry too much debt but will wait until they hit a cement wall before reacting. *Carpe diem!* It's like someone with a weight problem going on a diet only once the scale hits 350 pounds.

Being able to afford something should mean being able to cover all your obligations as a responsible adult. Okay, I know, I know—that's a fairly fluid concept.

The life of a responsible adult is filled with financial obligations: RRSPs, TFSAs, RESPs, life insurance, disability insurance, electricity, Internet, rent or mortgage, municipal taxes, groceries, and so forth. But after these are taken care of, how we spend our money comes down to priorities, lifestyle and risk tolerance.

Some believe it's more important to take a big trip every year than to secure their children's future. Others close their eyes and cross their fingers—"I better not have an accident on my bike or on the ski hill"—even if it means being penniless the day the unforeseen happens. Everyone has their own priorities and is responsible for their own life choices.

The question remains: what does it mean to be able to afford something?

You have to go back to your goals. Do you want to throw caution to the wind and have the unexpected hit you like a two-by-four in the face at twenty below zero? If so, sure, you can afford anything, but you need to know how to handle financial setbacks. Because they will come.

The most difficult thing with the concept of living in the now is not knowing what we will want tomorrow. The person I am today—"me now"—takes $20 chunks away from "future me," the person I will become.

What will "future me" want? What type of life will he lead? What kind of misfortunes will befall him? Will the nice straight line take an unwelcome detour? I am the person who's most responsible for the path my life takes.

The timing of cash coming in and going out is never perfect. Life is such that needs do not always match available liquidity. So you have two choices: being short on cash or planning ahead. In the planning curve of life, having ready cash in your bank account may be the leeway you need in five or ten years.

From theory to practice

Let's take the example of an amateur snowboarder. He already has two snowboards, the value of which greatly exceeds his talent. He goes into a store and sees a new object of desire: the Burton board that Shaun White uses.

During the day, he works in an office. He earns $45,000 per year. He doesn't contribute enough to his RRSP, and his two children are in elementary school and don't have RESPs, and the amateur snowboarder is getting more and more frustrated.

Basically, the $2,000 currently showing on his bank statement is the money he wants to use to buy the board. The problem is that the money is there because it hasn't been transferred to his RRSP for the year (he makes his contribution in January when his adviser calls, but he also reins in the amount of his contribution, because he "can't afford" to put aside much right now).

If he were to factor in his goals and obligations, his account would show a negative balance of $15,000. How so? Because outgoing payments await him, even though they aren't in his immediate field of vision: an RRSP contribution, roof repairs, a car payment, signing his youngest up for hockey, and so on. Even so, he buys the snowboard "because he can afford it." He sees the cash he has on hand without considering that it is already earmarked for something else.

Being able to afford it means being able to go into the office one morning, write your letter of resignation and leave at 9:23, for good. Being able to afford it gives you the freedom to move, act and be. It is a little cash in the *carpe diem* account (or, as one article called it, the *fuck off fund*[1]).

What being able to afford it truly means is being able to leave everything at a moment's notice. The point is not that you actually do it, but that you are able to do it. So you can afford an expense once all the other essential items, like the *carpe diem* account, have been taken care of.

The average

In theory, when you earn an average salary, you don't have much financial leeway. Why? Because in a balanced market, at the intersection of supply and demand, we get a fair price for a good or service: the limit of the average person's ability to pay. As a

---

1   www.thebillfold.com (search *A Story of a Fuck Off Fund*)

result, average people will be perpetually short of cash if they don't make rational choices.

People who earn more can afford to drive up prices. Let's take the example of a home purchase in Montreal. A number of buyers show up for an open house. Nine potential buyers present an offer at the upper limit of what they can afford, between $350,000 and $375,000. Then a tenth potential buyer raises the stakes and offers $400,000. Will the nine other buyers make the irrational choice of raising their initial offer, or will they simply look in another "less desirable" neighbourhood?

Many first-time home buyers experience this phenomenon as the law of supply and demand rears its head. The average Joe or Josephine is practically forced to live at the edge of his or her means.

The question of the future changes how you look at things. You may be able to afford it today, but tomorrow you won't. Or vice versa. Maybe your cash flow is limited right now, but tomorrow you'll have more . . . not to mention more needs.

A relative concept

There is no way of definitively determining whether you can afford something. It's a question of perception and goals. For example, if you are prepared to eat Kraft Dinner three hundred days a year, you create the leeway to eat something better the rest of the time. But who's willing to do that?

Similarly, some people are prepared to live in poverty from age sixty-five to ninety-five in exchange for a youth spent living it up. Everyone has their goals; what is important is that people be aware of their choices and the consequences of them.

Basically, numbers don't have any absolute meaning, but they have to be ambitious and realistic enough to represent your life in ten, twenty and thirty years. Having a financial strategy that is set in stone based on your needs at age twenty is like wanting to own a video store for the next thirty years: nothing is definitive.

As for the neighbours whose credit looks like a balloon filled with the helium of spending, often they don't ask themselves any questions; their appearance-based reality tends to be at the mercy of unexpected events. A helium-filled balloon eventually deflates.[1]

You may be starting to wonder what it means to be able to afford something, if, in a relative world, it can mean anything and everything. You probably want me to take a position. Fine, here goes:

Generally speaking, being able to afford something means having planned for the expected AND the unexpected. It doesn't mean being cautious to the extreme, but being aware that the financial decisions we make today can have consequences that last far longer than we imagine.

For example, can I afford this trip, or is it eating up my children's tuition? Can I afford this sports car, or am I sentencing myself to four years of overtime and the resulting depression? Can I afford a marble shower, or am I spending money from the emergency leaky roof fund?

Some people will say, "Yes, but you only live once!" That's true, but that's the case for all consumers, which means that not every desire can be satisfied.

---

1   Movie recommendation: *The Joneses,* a 2009 American dramatic comedy directed by Derrick Borte.

Do you really need to be able to afford it? It's important to live your life, but under what conditions and at what cost? A man once told me, "I'm rich. I don't have any debt." That was a simple way of saying that he didn't owe anyone anything. So he could afford his freedom, but not his future obligations.

The game of money isn't necessarily easy. It often means deciding between having a Coke or a glass of water. It's all a matter of choice (whether or not you choose to make one).

LOVE
DO YOU REALLY NEED IT?

L ove. True love. We all want it (at least I think we do). Yes, we really need it, that one-way drive down Happiness Lane.

Love comes in many shapes: emotions, friendship, desire, sharing, compromise, experience, sex, forgiveness, openness, reproduction (for better or for worse), and so on. Love is a little bit of all of that and so much more.

Being loved is like getting a letter every day that says, "I want you in my life." Obviously, there are different degrees of love, and it takes different forms depending on the individual. Some will never have enough, and others will get too much. And yet others won't get the chance to experience it even a little.

The distribution of love is a bit like the distribution of wealth in our society: a tiny part of the population is born with a silver spoon of love in their mouth, whereas others will fight their whole lives just to get their share. What is the connection to personal finance? It takes a lot of love to survive financial life. Yes, love is f?%$?%$ financial. In fact, there is nothing more financial than love.

The couple: a financial relationship

"Hey, Accountant Dude! Quit confusing money with love. Love is not money. It's emotion!"

True . . . At first, it's just about feelings.

But when you start a life together, financial matters rear their head with a vengeance. Rationality has to be taken into account. Life becomes the day-to-day financial reality: you share car payments, rent, electricity, expenses for kids, and more. You do things as a couple. You travel together. You renovate the kitchen together. You plan together. You spend together, and you develop your savings strategy together.

Couples share not only costs but also investments and risk. **Basically, your spouse is a partner in love but also in business.** Your lifestyle and choices influence your personal and shared financial reality.

Couples don't necessarily become a brand like Kanye and Kim. "What?! Kanye and Kim aren't a brand!" You don't think so? So how is it that you know who I'm talking about? Because they have created a brand that extends beyond their relationship; their brand image has become bigger than their life together.

Kim is the glamorous socialite and entrepreneur, and Kanye is the bombastic rapper who attracts attention for his outrageous behaviour. It's Kanye and Kim, brand image. But I'm digressing. You don't need to have that sort of market value for your relationship to be financial.

It is, de facto.

The early days

There was a time when people met in real life and got to know each other gradually. These days, many people meet virtually and complete the love transaction in the real world.

No matter what the scenario, no matter what the platform, love is a transaction. It's a question of balance in the market: people who have the same love value on the love market end up forming short- or long-term unions, if they choose to.

How much is one person worth?

How about the other?

Not in money, but in love value. When the two values are similar, there is a chance of forming a couple. There's a lid for every pot, as the old saying goes.

So far, we've been talking about value on the love market. But pretty early on in the process of getting together, questions will start being asked to get a sense of the other person's finances. Do you want proof? No one will be so bold as to ask, "Are you rich?" or "How much do you make?" Naturally, the discussion will be much more subtle.

What do you do for a living?

What kind of car do you drive?

What neighbourhood do you live in?

Where do you like to go on holiday?

What's your favourite restaurant?

These types of indirect questions are a subtle way of teasing out financial information. For example, the difference between "company president" and "convenience store clerk" gives a pretty good idea of your standard of living. Dinner at a five-star establishment costs the same as an entire year of french fries at Swiss Chalet. What you make of the answers to these "innocent" conversation starters depends on the importance of financial criteria in your current hierarchy of values.

WHEN MONEY KILLS LOVE

Once a relationship is formed, you need to agree on the lifestyle you want and can afford. One day, a colleague came into my office, his spirits as low as the pile on the office's cheap carpet. Our job descriptions were worlds apart, but he respected my work and I respected his.

He confided in me that his relationship was on the financial rocks. He and his wife urgently needed to get their finances in order. Their mortgage had climbed to more than the original price of the house. Like many couples, they had eaten into the equity of the house year after year to pay off consumer debt.

Basically, the couple was spending the equity in the house. They had run out of leeway. My colleague was aware of this and wanted to address the problem, but his wife didn't want to. It was the end of the road for them. Obviously, they had other problems, but with such pressing financial concerns, the boat ended up sinking.

Much more than sharing expenses

When you are part of a couple, you need to agree on what kind of shared lifestyle you want. By clarifying each person's expectations at the outset (see "Managing Expectations: Do You Really Need To?" on page 248), you avoid plenty of conflict, even though other conflicts are bound to arise pretty soon.

People sometimes think that a simple agreement on how expenses should be shared is sufficient. It's not, because finances can become a permanent source of frustration between partners, particularly when they live together. Of course, life goals can change along the way, but basically you need to be on the same page regarding financial principles for the medium and long term. Here are a few examples:

- ✔ *Debt.* How much debt is acceptable to both parties? Will a certain lifestyle keep my partner up at night?
- ✔ *Annual savings goals.* What is our annual savings goal? What percentage of our salaries needs to be put aside? Should we save for an RRSP, for an RESP or to do renovations?
- ✔ *Neighbourhood.* What kind of lifestyle do we want? A place in the suburbs or the excitement of city life? A small, simple apartment, or a house with three bathrooms?
- ✔ *Children.* Do we really want them? If we do, now we need to know how many to have (see "Children: Do You Really Need Them?" on page 184). Some people say that you shouldn't decide on how many children to have based on budget; let them tell that to my grandfather Anatole and my grandmother Léona, who had thirteen children, not to mention several miscarriages.
- ✔ *Spending.* What will be considered personal expenses and what will be shared expenses? Is saving to buy a snowmobile really a shared project? Should that be financed from the family budget?
- ✔ *Power struggles.* If there is a considerable income gap between the two partners, the issue of power needs to be addressed. It's too easy to say, "I contribute more financially, so I have the final say," whether implicitly or explicitly. If the income gap is wide, this conversation will arise naturally.

✔ *Dreams.* Realizing your dreams is important. We all need to find fulfillment, but in a relationship there is no guarantee that your dreams and the other person's dreams will be the same. If one dreams of living in New York and the other can't imagine leaving their hometown, the financial planning won't be the same. Can the two dreams be reconciled?

These are just a few examples of topics that need to be addressed.

How do you share expenses?

This is a thorny topic. It's a major bone of contention for couples, according to surveys in supermarket tabloids (and some serious publications as well). Contrary to what you may think, there is no one answer to this question. There are a number of ways to approach the issue. Here is one, just to get the argument started.

First off, here is a financial love continuum. Where is your relationship on it?

Each their fair share　　　　　　**All for one and one for all**

At the beginning of a relationship, "each their fair share" is understandable. But when marriage, children or a long-term relationship are in the cards, normally people move toward "All for one and one for all." Obviously, if you are wealthy, it is a good idea to meet with a family lawyer to find out about the financial and legal implications of marriage.

Each their fair share. This is an agreement whereby a couple benefits from economies of scale for shared expenses, and where the breakdown of payments is based on a method agreed upon by both parties.

> **Pro**: There is less sense of unfairness in the event of a separation, and property is more easily split. There is a connection between effort expended and value obtained.

> **Con:** Carefully tracking expenses can grow tiresome and demanding, and be a source of conflict. When love morphs into spreadsheet management, couple time may suffer.

All for one and one for all. Under this agreement, a couple is a single entity. Income and expenses are merged and handled as a single financial person.

> **Pro**: Simpler to manage.

> **Con:** There is tremendous potential for conflict when the spouses don't agree on what is an acceptable expense versus an unacceptable one. There is a risk of abuse, intentional or not, by one of the partners.

My observation: I think a flexible position is the best solution. At the beginning, you need to manage your financial relationship as if you were roommates (each their fair share), and then move to all for one and one for all when the first child is born or when another event requires a particular commitment (for example, if one spouse decides to start a business, which could be the couple's financial making or their undoing).

Defining "each their fair share"

The concept of "fair share" depends on perceptions of what is fair, spending habits and each person's financial situation.

The 50/50 split

Splitting everything 50/50 may seem fair for certain expenses. When you're single, you need a place to live. So splitting the rent 50/50 makes sense if each person's portion is lower than what they would be spending if they were living alone. The same can apply to heating, telecommunications and other joint expenses.

But if the couple moves into a house or apartment that is not affordable for one of them, they should probably contribute different amounts. The person who wants to live in the more upscale neighbourhood should pay more if the other can't afford it.

A percentage of salary?

Why not split expenses as a percentage of each person's salary? Unless both partners' salaries are stable, this could lead to nonstop arguments. Which salary should be used as a basis? Gross? The average tax rate isn't the same. Net? Does one of the people earn part of their money under the table? Do you include a pension plan in total compensation?

If one spouse contributes to a defined contribution pension plan and the other doesn't have an employer's pension plan, what is the share of the RRSP that should be deducted from income to calculate the reference salary? These questions can be a colossal pain. Throw children from a blended family into the mix and figuring out what constitutes a fair share can be a real head-scratcher.

I'm raising a lot of questions and not providing answers. That is intentional. **It's up to each person to analyze their situation and determine how they feel about their financial contribution as part of the couple.**

Imagine a situation in which one of the spouses is an entrepreneur and is drawing a low salary, by choice, reinvesting the surplus in the business. Or they may have a variable income with peaks and valleys.

For example, one year that person decides to draw a salary of $50,000, while the following year he or she decides instead to take a $20,000 dividend and leave the surplus in the business. What income is used for the calculation? Sounds like an argument brewing to me.

Based on each person's spending?

Who downloaded the most on the Internet this month? How is it possible for one person to download so much? Did both partners use the Internet? Who ate out more? Who treated themselves more? Who takes the longer shower? Who eats more ketchup, buys more beer or drinks more wine?

This is an approach to splitting expenses that can only create conflict. At the same time, it raises the concept of user-pay, and the tracking involved in this method is difficult and cumbersome, on top of being a virtually guaranteed death knell for love. "You have to pay for that condom. Why? Because you came and I didn't!" (#humour)

How do you compensate for unpaid work?

Imagine the following scenario: One of the partners does all the housework, errands and cooking while holding down a paying job. The other makes a minimal contribution to cleaning but makes a lot of money. If one person spends their free time renovating the house, sparing no effort, how much is that worth? How do you quantify each person's contribution if you want to be fair? Just this paragraph alone has thrown a Molotov cocktail into the idea of financial harmony.

The case of transportation

Transportation is a good example. Let's say a couple buys a car but one of the partners uses it mainly for work. Outside of working hours, the car is used by both of them to varying degrees depending on the week. Plus, the spouse who doesn't use the car for work uses public transit to get around. How do you split the expense?

The answer depends on a lot of things. For instance, was it a mutual decision to live near one person's place of work but far from the other's? Once you start asking such questions, it does make it harder to split expenses equitably.

Household transportation needs to be seen as a whole. Expenses related to the car, bike sharing and public transit passes should all be shared in a way that makes sense. Who pays what? How much and why? Joint decisions influence what each person pays.

FINANCIAL INDEPENDENCE

A mother warns her daughter[1]: "Never depend on anyone financially. Make sure you have the power to make choices and that you don't have to deal with financial problems you didn't ask for."

Wise words indeed. The mother doesn't want her daughter to rely on anyone else to be able to live her life; she doesn't want anyone to make her decisions for her. She doesn't want her daughter to have to beg for what she wants or have to ask anyone's permission to live the life of her dreams. This may be a message from a mother who didn't have the power herself to negotiate on equal terms.

I once received an e-mail from a woman who wrote, "I couldn't afford to leave my husband, but I did it anyway." In the name of true love, we often lose sight of a simple fact: it's important to hold on to one's independence and to have the financial wherewithal to leave a situation that's no longer tenable.

In the event of a separation: protecting your partner

Taking into account the possibility of a separation doesn't mean you love each other any less. It shows that you are being realistic; that you have the sense to look around you and see that, despite the best intentions, not everything comes up roses. I've seen a fair number of my friends split up recently. In addition to the resulting sadness, finances rear their head pretty quickly.

How do you split your belongings? Who will have the kids more often? How much will alimony be? What neighbourhood

---

1   I use a daughter in this example, but it could just as easily be a son.

will each person live in (taking into consideration the kids' schools and their friends)? Who gets to keep the car? Who gets to keep the house (if that's possible)? Who paid more for the house? Who provided the bigger down payment? The administrative complexity involved in separation shows the extent to which a couple has not just an emotional relationship but also, more than ever, a business relationship.

So . . . what have you planned in case you separate?

Do you each have your own investments?

Has one person been saving while the other pays the household expenses?

Did one person invest in a business while the other was spending more time taking care of the family?

One thing is sure: if you gave up your career to raise a family, unless you have a major windfall or are J.K. Rowling, you rarely manage to make up the gap between actual income and what you could have earned.

So, in the event of a separation, isn't taking a financial hit for the other person's benefit a kind of proof that your love actually existed? Obviously, if one person leaves to get together with the other's best friend, you can expect a battle of epic proportions.

Not convinced yet?

Still think a relationship is a question of emotion and only emotion?

Is your spouse insured in the event of an untimely death? Who is the beneficiary of the policy?

Did you contribute to your spouse's RRSP?

Did you know that upon one spouse's death, the other spouse gets certain tax benefits?

And if your spouse fritters away your financial future, it's no problem, right? Of course it is!

Love may be blind, but the bank account isn't.

This chapter may have the effect of bursting your romantic bubble and dispelling the idea that you can live on love alone. The fact is, you are never in complete control of a romantic relationship. It gets worn down day by day, and the wonderful feelings of the past can make way for the disenchantment of time passing. The relationship can end against your will or by your own hand.

However, you can see problems on the horizon and manage your romantic life. Because if you love each other, you don't want to leave each other in poverty. You have to love each other enough to financially cushion the potential sorrow if love should fade.

There is no one way to share finances in a relationship. You just have to be comfortable with how things are calculated and be willing to revisit the discussion later on.

So, do you really need love? Of course! Love is what makes our time on this earth meaningful. Get out there and find it, wherever it is.

And financially managing that love? Even more important!

NB: This chapter does not consider the legal aspects of relationships, because family law and taxation are highly complex. Couples should find out about the legal implications of their decisions, because they can have major financial consequences, particularly if they separate. What you may believe is reality may not be what the law requires.

A JOB
DO YOU REALLY NEED IT?

U nless you are the heir to a family fortune, most people have to work for a living.

Do you have to keep the same job your whole life?

Can you eventually turn your hobby into your job?

Do you have to do the same kind of work your entire life?

This chapter demonstrates the importance of creating your own market value so you can eventually make the shift from worker to investor. Once you have become an investor, you can dream about your pension. That's the financial structure of our society.

As your body ages, you move from the active population to the retiree population. Once the body is no longer able to keep up and loses its market value, you need to have accumulated a pension. That's a fact of life.

Start somewhere

June 1996.

I'm almost seventeen years old, and I'm headed home with my McDonald's cap and shirt. This is my first real job; a company agreed to hire me and pay me $6.10 an hour. It took me a little while to become productive, but after a few shifts I got the hang of things. Actually, I don't know whether I kept increasing my productivity or whether I just found a way to keep going faster safely.

What some people saw as a job, I saw as a sport: there are rules, you need to perform, and you need to learn. What did I learn today? That's the question I've asked myself in every job I've ever held, in any activity I've engaged in, and on every day of school. Am I wasting my time or developing something new? Am I repeating myself or consolidating what I know?

Your first job is important; it has an influence on those that follow. Choosing a job that is demanding and perceived as such is an investment in your CV. At first, you work for starvation wages. The ultimate goal is to stop working for minimum wage. Instead, work for a result and greater intrinsic value than just putting in time. You have to develop your ability to become an investor.

My goal has always been to one day be paid for intangible value, expertise or market value, not based on the time put into a job. Thinking of your life in terms of hours worked is a labourer's vision of work.

Putting in time doesn't necessarily confer value on the job done. What has value is what is produced or created over a period of time. For example, the fact that you spend four hours painting a wall with meticulous care does not impart greater value to the wall, in the client's eyes, than if the same wall was painted in thirty minutes. This is why clients don't want to pay by the hour and would rather pay based on results. The difference in time between the two scenarios gives the client no added value. So why maintain the mentality of hourly pay?

Shifting from employee to investor: a necessary mix

Once you start working, you need to think like an investor. Why? Because cash goes out faster than it comes in. There is a gap between incoming and outgoing funds. Believing that you will be able to meet your obligations with that week's pay amounts to ignorance of where you want to be financially.

 Certain expenses, like those related to education or retirement, have to be planned, which is another reason why you need to think like an investor. And to invest, you need to save money.

The fundamental error young working people make is spending or rewarding themselves before investing. That amounts to thinking like a poor person. It should be the exact opposite. Spending should come from what's left in the budget after you invest.

Investing in your education so you don't feel like you're working

When you start out, you may invest in your studies. But are you really increasing your market value by studying in your chosen field? I can already hear a certain philosophy professor of mine labelling me a utilitarian advancing neoliberal interests. I'll let him have his fun and throw shade my way: the teaching of philosophy doesn't make you exempt from specious arguments.

These days, does it make sense to study for the sake of knowledge? Doesn't the widespread availability of information mean that we no longer have to pay professors to regurgitate what books already say? For instance, I don't need a bachelor's degree in philosophy to read John Rawls's *A Theory of Justice*, particularly if I have no intention of teaching the topic.

Essentially, if you study in a field where the degree does not let others know that you have useful professional expertise, do you really need a degree? Knowledge is never useless. But a degree is an accreditation; it is testimony to qualifications and skills. If you don't intend to, or don't have the opportunity to, use it professionally, do you really need it?

The question always boils down to the same one: how will this investment increase my value and happiness? And don't forget the goal, which is to go from a worker to a person of private means. Will my education contribute to that?

It may surprise some to hear the question asked, but is it a good idea to spend years at university studying in a field where the prospects lead straight to the same place as secretarial school? In terms of financial investments, it just doesn't make sense.

There'll be those who say, "Yes, but life is about more than just money!" That's absolutely true. But it takes money, and lots of it, to enjoy certain experiences. Getting a university education without thinking about where it will lead is a questionable investment with major financial consequences.

When I hear university graduates complain about being unemployed despite having a master's degree, I always wonder why they chose to study what they did. Anyone can—and should—consult the employment statistics related to every programme.

If you don't think you will be the best in a given area of expertise or be able to carve out a niche for yourself, why devote such significant financial resources to it? Investing financially in an education means investing in your human capital.

Obviously, there are always people who are the exception to the rule, who use their degree in an unusual way. Let's take the example of the popular illusionist Luc Langevin. He uses his knowledge of physics to perform magic tricks (or optical physics tricks). He managed to combine his degree in science with his artistic aspirations, even though it's not the usual path someone with this type of education would follow.

It's important to find a field that suits you and that lets you do what you love. I'm not talking about choosing something easy, but rather a field of study you are passionate about. That's no small feat at age eighteen or twenty.

If you find a path you are passionate about, your work won't feel like work. **Aspiring to love your work is still a commendable and realistic goal.** For many people, it's the futile quest for nirvana; for others, it's non-negotiable.

Making the leap

School teaches us how to be employees. It delivers labour to employers. When you talk to career counsellors or go to job fairs, you are being sold openings, salaries and working conditions.

I don't remember meeting many entrepreneurs through school. Being an entrepreneur doesn't just mean trading in things. George Clooney, Beyoncé and Drake are all entrepreneurs in their own way: they have created cultural value from what they know and their inventiveness.

As an entrepreneur, you need to work. Every minute devoted

to work hones your entrepreneurial vision and increases its value. But be careful if you're thinking of getting into the restaurant business. It looks better than it is: crazy hours, intense competition and a significant risk of failure.

Going into business for the sake of going into business isn't a good idea. You need to have the conviction that what you are offering has value and that you can protect that value over the long term and make it profitable.

Entrepreneurship isn't for everyone, but an investment in time and money is required for most. You have to learn to invest, move beyond your mentality as a payer and try to develop the mentality of a receiver. Which brings us back to the heart of it: is becoming your own boss a necessary step toward becoming an investor?

Earning money while you sleep

The goal when you invest in the stock market or a private company is to generate a return while you're spending time on something else. Becoming an investor means making money while you sleep. If you own an income property that you paid a fair price for, it technically generates a return at night too. The tenants are sleeping, but they are paying you to occupy the space while they rest.

It's the same for stock market investments: while you're doing other things, your money is working for you. This seems out of reach at age sixteen, but it becomes the norm at fifty and an implicit obligation at around sixty-five or seventy. And no, retirement isn't a time to rest. It's a time when most people go from worker to investor. Our minds and bodies may no longer be working for money, but our money is still working for us.

Working: a changing concept

So, do you need to keep working? Yes, if you have never been an investor. It seems obvious, but it's a life's work to make the shift from worker to investor at the right time. And a lot of people don't take this seriously.

If you defer investing, you pay for it down the line. Prioritizing fun over investing is a mistake, because the money you spend when you're young, supposedly on fun, will have a negative impact on your quality of life in the decades that follow. **A sports car purchased in your twenties represents a down payment on a house at the beginning of your thirties.** Don't forget, the things we do have repercussions.

In a 2014 report on RRSP contributions, Statistics Canada noted: "Nationally, the median contribution was $2,930, a 3.5% increase from 2011. The median is the point at which half of the contributors contributed more than $2,930 and half less."[1]

Given the level of RRSP contributions, will Canadians be able to make the shift from workers to investors? It seems unlikely. With low returns on the stock market, you need more and more capital to become a full-time investor when you retire. And this is set against a backdrop of life expectancies that continue to rise.

Today's investors have three priorities. They need to:

1. **save more capital**, because returns will be lower in the future than in the past, and the retirement period will likely be longer;
2. **take more risks** to get returns on par with those of the previous generation; and
3. **invest over a longer period.**

---

1   http://www.statcan.gc.ca/daily-quotidien/140325/dq140325b-eng.htm

A job: do you really need it? If you don't want to invest and have your money work for you, the answer is yes.

I'm not pushing the idea of getting rich, just doing your best with what you have. Once you're an investor, there is nothing to stop you from working for pleasure after you retire, whether to pass the time or to bring home the bacon. Isn't that what true freedom is, after all?

But you should ask another question: what makes you think you will still be employable at sixty-five, seventy or seventy-five? Canadians sure love playing Russian roulette . . .

NEW STUFF
DO YOU REALLY NEED IT?

"I love it! It has that new car smell!"

Hmmm ... not only is that "new" smell generally the result of volatile organic compounds, which are considered toxic, but we also seem to be obsessed with new things, not just cars. It's as though being the first to use something substantially increases its value.

There is also a major disconnect between the price you pay for something new and the actual utility and satisfaction it delivers. The main advantage of buying something new is its immediate availability, but you pay dearly for that availability. Something strange happens: even though, when we opt for something used, we improve our quality of life in a more economical way, we can't stop thinking we "deserve" new things.

But it's not a question of deserving; it's a question of knowing how much you have in the bank. Rich kids don't "deserve" to spend all that they spend. They just have the means to do so.

Used goods are for poor people!

Wealth and used goods create cognitive dissonance. Since we aspire to wealth (or at least to less poverty), we seem to think that if we have the money to buy new, then buying new should be our first reflex. But one of the most sensible economic choices you can make is to buy second-hand.

Why? Because the price of a used good drops more quickly than its utility. A new hammer costs $25, but you can pick one up at a garage sale for $3. Can it still pound nails like when it was brand new? Of course. Often, the answer to that sort of question is yes. The drop in price is not proportional to the product's utility.

With websites and classified apps that put buyers in touch with sellers day or night, it is hard to argue that looking for something used requires much effort. Generally, someone somewhere is trying to sell what you're trying to buy.

Plus, since looking for used goods takes time, I automatically make the connection with a spending strategy (see "A Spending Strategy: Do You Really Need It?" on page 243): while I search for the thing I want, I have time to let the idea of buying such a thing sit, and then I can make the decision whether or not to buy it. When it comes to spending, your worst enemy is being in a rush, and your best friend is time.

If you aspire to be less poor and have a good standard of living, your main priority should be to stop buying new and take advantage of all the things people are selling that used to be objects of desire, and that are now used.

Buying used means getting things cheaper than they would be if bought new; also, you don't have to pay sales tax to the neighbour who's selling a lawn mower. Buying used lets you compare the value of things with their utility.

Let's take the example of dining room furniture. A set that would cost $4,000 in the store will inevitably be sold off in a garage sale. Fortunately, although things lose their value, they maintain their usefulness.

So when you feel like getting new dining room furniture, even though you eat perfectly well on the set you have, forget the IKEA catalogue and home decor magazines. Instead, you should try to find someone who is also looking for a new table and wants to sell theirs.

Buying a new table is too expensive and you don't really need it. Seriously, do you want to work for weeks at an average salary for a dining room set that will soon have lost its lustre anyway?

Don't forget that things are no longer new the moment they're unwrapped. Do you really need to be the first one to unwrap them?

LEARNING FROM MISTAKES

I've bought a lot of things new, particularly guitars. If I had it to do over again, would I do the same? Probably not. I'm one of those weekend musicians with only the mirror or children wandering around my house as an audience.

Guitars last a lifetime, so why not buy the object of your desire from a musician who mistook himself for Jimi Hendrix? Classified ads are filled with guitars being sold by musicians who are broke or who have turned a page in their lives.

Getting things repaired: back to basics

In addition to wanting to buy new, another reflex of a consumer society is to throw things out rather than get them repaired. Go ahead. Throw it out. It costs less to buy new than to have something old repaired. Really?

It's true that lots of goods, particularly electronics, are designed not to be repaired, or so that the cost of repair is higher than the value of the thing new, made in China.

Still, some things can be repaired—take bikes, for example. The other day a friend spent $150 to restore his 1990s bike. An equivalent bike would cost $500 plus tax today. As a result, he has a working bike, his needs have been met, and he saved a few hundred dollars.

This clever approach applies to many things: cars, patio sets, barbecues, loveseats, coffee tables, bedroom furniture and much more. The propensity to replace things that are still useful but that need to be repaired or want a bit of TLC shows people how rich we are . . . or that we don't know the value of money.

Shoes are another good example. With successive visits to Payless ShoeSource, we end up throwing out what we bought there. But changing a heel or a sole or using a bit of polish can make all the difference to a pair of shoes originally thought ready for the trash heap.

The same apples to jackets with broken zippers (remember the one I've been wearing for thirteen years with the defective slider? See "Listening to Other People: Do You Really Need To?" on page 69). After one YouTube video and a $5 online purchase, you'll get a few more years out of the jacket. Does it still keep you warm? Does it still protect against rain and snow? Oh, wait—you've had it for years? So what? Are you afraid of people thinking you're not fashionable?

Obviously, you don't just get something repaired for the sake of it; you have to run the numbers. The golden rule is that the repair should buy the object years of life and avoid a big expense. For instance, if you get something worth $500 repaired for $200, you have to make sure the outlay makes sense. Even though the item is old, if repairing it means you won't have to shell out the extra $300 plus tax for five years, you've just bought yourself time, and therefore money.

Buying time

Buying used buys time. Let's say someone nets $1,000 every two weeks. When that person pays $500 for a used item rather than $1,000 for the same thing new, he or she has just saved the equivalent of one week of vacation time.

Buying used allows the person to get the item sooner, because he or she needs to save only $500 net rather than the $1,000 for the new thing. This approach:

✔ postpones shelling out the amount equal to the difference between the cost of the new good and the cost of buying something second-hand; and
✔ lets you own and use the thing sooner.

This logic applies perfectly to consumer durables, because certain used items last as long as new stuff. Dining room furniture is a great example: unless there is a fire or something breaks, a used set can last a lifetime, just like a brand new set.

Kids' stuff

 Kids are an endless source of wealth for retailers. Everything made for them is too expensive and is used for a limited time.

It's a trap: they play on parents' love for their children to sell them stuff they don't need. And yet, almost everything kids need can be found used.

Why buy a new sled for kids?

Why do you need a crib that matches the nursery?

A new bike? I hope you're kidding, because kids' bikes last only one or two summers. The same applies to skates, toys and clothing.

Parents who pay the bills will eventually see the light and stop equating money spent with love for their children. They will buy used clothes in bulk rather than one thing at a time. They will hand the first child's toys down to the second. They will even gift-wrap toys the first child used a few years earlier. I've bought my sons a lot of new books. The person who eventually buys the contents of their bookshelves will be getting a gold mine at a fraction of the price.

FREE TIP!

Don't be shy to tell a parent who has closed the reproductive chapter of their life that you will take everything off their hands for $1,000. Plenty of parents would be happy to put all the cloth diapers, clothes, toys, furniture and everything else together to avoid having to sell things one by one.

And don't forget that buying things used can correspond with an increase in needs. So you can have your in-laws' old dining table for twenty years and wait till you are more comfortable financially to buy a new one. But you could also restore it to give it a second life. Why not?

In a society where personal and collective debt is more than $22,837,[1] buying used goods can be a lifesaver. Before you struggle to earn an extra $400 in taxable income per year, couldn't you look at how you're spending and cut in the expense column?

New stuff: do you really need it? Keep in mind that the void you are trying to fill by buying things new will never be filled. It's a bottomless pit.

---

1   https://www.consumer.equifax.ca/about-equifax/press-releases/-/blogs/
total-canadian-consumer-debt-climbs-to-over-1-8-trillion-but-delinquencies-and-
bankruptcies-edge-down

OWNERSHIP
DO YOU REALLY NEED IT?

I s it really important to own things? People accumulate things throughout their lives. The older we get, the more moving our stuff becomes an epic, tedious exercise. Is there a better approach to ownership?

The glorification of stuff

From childhood, we glorify owning stuff. We ask children what they want for their birthday. Implicitly, we are asking them what stuff they want to own. This positions things that are purchased as something rare, encouraging children to consider new possessions as a reward that comes with birthdays or special events.

Children grow up with this idea, and as they age, they want to keep rewarding themselves. Their attachment to things shows in the way they talk: "That's MY truck," or "MY bike." Why are humans so attached to their stuff?

I don't have the answer.

Collecting: an aberration that supposedly makes sense

Collecting. It's a strange pastime, isn't it? When people collect things, they feel pride in establishing the collection, preserving it and organizing it.

When I was young, I collected hockey cards. I was attracted by the resale value of the cards. But to sell them, you need a buyer. Twenty-five years later, I can tell you that few people care about Kevin Hatcher's or Joe Sakic's rookie card. Particularly since those old hockey cards were printed in such big runs that they never achieved the value that was touted back then.

Then I got into music. With my passion for music, I collected around 1,800 records over twenty-five years, which cost thousands of dollars. Almost all of those albums are now available for just a few dollars a month with a monthly subscription to Google Play or a similar service.

My goal wasn't to collect CDs. I just wanted to listen to what I wanted to listen to, without having to call in to a radio station, like Carole from Laval asking the host to play Martin Stevens's "Love Is in the Air."

It no longer makes economic sense to own music the way it used to. Music is everywhere and can be heard inexpensively. Artists may not be happy, but the business model has changed.

Eventually, collections of any sort will stop making sense. Can you really find long-term meaning from accumulating stuff? That's a highly personal question.

Poverty and accumulating stuff

It's easy to say that you have to get rid of possessions, but it's hard to rationalize from a certain point of view. **Living in an uncluttered house is a luxury afforded to the well-off.** Why? Because

FREE TIPS!

1. **The three-year rule**

   I've made a rule for myself: If I haven't used an object in three years, it's likely that I've kept it for no reason. So I can consider getting rid of it.

2. **Moving**

   Every move raises questions about what should be kept and what should be thrown out. Moving forces us to take stock of our stuff and get rid of things we don't need.

3. **Life in limited space**

   The amount of living space you have forces you to think before buying something. When the opportunity to buy something big arises, ask yourself where it's going to go. Most of the time, the purchase gets postponed.

4. **New pushes out old**

   Say you buy a new book—what do you have around the house that you no longer need? By establishing a practice of things coming in and going out systematically, you force yourself to question owning a particular object.

they have the money to pay over and over for the same item and to get rid of it when it's damaged. People who live in poverty keep the extra possession for when it might come in handy.

To rent or to buy?

The eternal question: to rent or to buy? When I was renovating my duplex, I realized how much sense it makes to rent tools. There is a rental company a few minutes from my house that enables resource sharing. You can rent anything from an extension cord to a gas can.

Why buy and keep things you won't use often? Why buy ski equipment if you hit the slopes once a year or camping equipment for one night under the stars every five years? You can rent it all, even a sleeping bag. Similarly, does it really make sense for everyone in the neighbourhood to have their own lawn mower or pressure washer?

The cost of stuff
Once you have accumulated objects, you have to keep them, maintain them, clean them, store them, organize them, and so on. **Objects require shelves, storage and space**. How many square feet in your home is devoted to storing and containing objects? The answer may surprise you.

Much of the square footage in a house is devoted to maintaining objects in an enclosure of ownership. According to a 2014 *Los Angeles Times* article, the average American household owns 300,000 objects.[1] That seems like a lot, but it adds up quickly when you start to count.

When you buy a house in the suburbs with a basement, the amount of stuff you own can get out of control. Don't forget that if you are buying a house mainly to contain your stuff, you wind up renovating, heating and insuring rooms just to keep your things.

Is it possible to reduce the space we need by getting rid of some of our possessions? Are our homes too big? Limiting the size of your home requires that you limit the number of objects you bring home and store there.

Plus, if you followed the user guides for the things you buy,

---

1   articles.latimes.com/2014/mar/21/health/la-he-keeping-stuff-20140322

you would have to spend a lifetime maintaining them. Since time is limited, owning objects means spending part of your life taking care of them. And as the saying goes, time is money.

A LESSON FROM THE QUIET OLD GUY NEXT DOOR[1]

He would wave at me every morning. My 86-year-old neighbour ate his soup daily on his front steps. He was a nice guy who would ask me what was new while he watched me dig my basement by hand.

He sort of became part of my life. I like old people: their experience, their stories and their memories. I find them inspiring, because they built a different life, a different reality.

Then one morning he told me he wanted to sell his house.

He had resigned himself to the idea. It was time to move on. Moving one last time, bidding farewell to his life because "there's not as much time left as there used to be," as my uncle Maurice said at his last Christmas dinner.

A few hours later, I ran into my neighbour at the local ice cream parlour. A vanilla cone was part of his weekly routine. He invited me to visit his house.

All of a sudden I was transported back to 1979. In this scene from another era, only a microwave from 1998 and a Sharp cathode screen TV were anachronisms. There was no clutter, no attempt at decor. A rug covered part of the hardwood floor, and the walls were only one colour and stained from years of cigarette smoke. He had quit at some point along the way.

---

1   Revised version of an article initially published on the Voir.ca blog: voir.ca/pierre-yves-mcsween/2014/06/20/jaime-les-vieux

The man had never had the Internet, and he didn't think he was missing anything. But one thing in particular struck me: he didn't own any stuff. In the room he used as an office, he had only an empty desk made of metal and wood, which was a few decades old. Opening a closet door, he said, "These are my finances. They're a bit upside down." Two folders a few centimetres thick with papers in them was what he meant by "a bit upside down."

Sometimes older people seem to get by without owning useless stuff. Why own something that won't be useful until the end of our useful lives? For my neighbour, it wasn't a matter of not having the money; he sold his house for a song. "Why sell for more? I don't really need the money. I don't have any heirs, so what's the point in accumulating more?"

He was right.

After my visit, when I went back home, I was depressed by what a materialist I am. Why have all these useless objects, all these things that make us sick, that require maintenance, creating stress and taking up our time?

Why keep CD cases when only the music is important? Why keep books we won't read again? For an intellectual, a bookcase

 filled with books is like muscles to a gym rat: it's a physical way of showing off the result of our work. Giving away books and setting them free is a bit like letting go of the proof of our investment in knowledge.

The clothes you wore only once?

Wrapping paper? Are you really going to give fifty-four gifts this year?

Why hang on to that DVD, *The Making of* Die Hard? Who has time to watch the special features in the making of a Bruce Willis film?

The list of useless stuff is long, and our time is limited.

Old people are quietly teaching us something with the simplicity of their lives. But we don't really listen. When they lose their independence, we offer them a bath once a week and we decide that they aren't contributing. But in their own way, they are putting the brakes on the fast pace of life these days.

Yes, I like old people. Because they are, in a way, a mirror of our future.

At the end of our lives, shouldn't we be considered an asset, rather than being considered for our assets? When I'm that age, at least I'll have a few existential choices to make, like whether I want Jell-O or rice pudding for dessert.

If I had listened to my mother, I would have kept my Legos from 1990 to today. Of course, I would have loved to play with those Lego pieces with my sons. But by giving them away back when Hammer pants were cool, I allowed them to make other children happy for twenty-five years rather than collect dust on a shelf.

How many objects are kept for too long for no reason?

Keeping things is expensive. When you give them away, lend them, rent them or sell them, you make an impact on your personal finances. Because sound management of stuff sometimes involves borrowing, not owning. So, ownership: do you really need it? Not necessarily.

AN RESP
DO YOU REALLY NEED IT?

In Quebec in 2012, a series of protests and student strikes took place, in opposition to a proposed hike in university tuition fees. During one of those strikes, a television report described the difficult predicament of a mother, who expressed her dismay at how much a university education costs.

"How am I supposed to pay tens of thousands of dollars for three years for my children on an average family income?" she asked. The journalist left the question hanging.

To me, something about the statement didn't make sense. Since when do people wait for university to start before they begin planning for the expense? The news report made no mention of registered education savings plans.

I like to use the analogy of replacing the roof of your house. Let's say a new roof costs $10,000. Obviously, it's hard for the average person earning $40,000 a year to pay to replace their roof. Even if a household brings in two $40,000 salaries a year, a $10,000 roof is like a frying pan in the face for the family budget. That's why you need to save for major expenses every year to get out ahead of them. But when I say this, people often reply, "Come on, no one does that!"

No one? That's odd. Because when it comes to spending $25,000 on a car, even with an annual salary of around $40,000, many people don't raise an eyebrow. They buy it on monthly payments. So why not apply the same concept toward a child's education? It's not the same thing, you say?

We bring children into this world, and we pay for all manner of necessities and treats. But when they turn eighteen, those kids are entitled to ask what we have set aside for their education. If we reply, "Nothing," or "Very little," then we as parents have let them down. (Of course, I'm not referring to those on a very limited income: when you're in survival mode, it's hard to plan long-term for education.)

Don't leave free money on the table

Both provincial and federal governments offer benefits in the form of tax shelters and grants. All Canadians are entitled to the Canada Education Savings Grant, which represents a minimum of 20 percent of the amount contributed to an RESP if you are below the grant threshold. Federally, the Canadian grant can be up to 40 percent for the first $500 contributed to an RESP.

Despite evidence of this assurance of a minimum return, many people still leave money on the table. We complain about low stock market returns, but when we have a chance to jump on a minimum 20 percent free return, we take a pass.

You probably don't even need to contribute more than $2,500 a year to an RESP, since the grant maxes out when you reach that threshold. Tax optimization is achieved at $2,500 a year, or $208.33 a month.

At this maximum frequency, if you contribute $208.33 a month to an RESP for a little over fourteen years, you reach the cumulative maximum for grants in the fifteenth year of contributions. The maximum grant from the federal government is $7,200, for total contributions of $36,000. Other provinces may have supplementary grants, so it's worth it to inform yourself.

For low-income families, the federal government adds a bonus: the Canada Learning Bond. Even if a family didn't contribute one cent to a child's RESP, the government could grant up to $2,000: $500 when an RESP is opened and $100 a year until the calendar year the child turns fifteen.

Are you part of a low-income family? Why not check whether you're leaving money on the table? Why pass up free money? All you have to do is inform yourself a little and open an RESP. That's what I call time well invested.

RESPs have many advantages:

- ✔ When money is withdrawn, it is declared on the student's income tax return. Since a student's income is limited, there is little or no tax to pay.
- ✔ Tax on returns is deferred during contribution years: the money grows tax sheltered.
- ✔ The capital belongs to the parent contributing to the RESP.
- ✔ The returns and the grant belong to the student.

The way I see it, people who "invest" $500 or more in a handbag rather than opening an RESP for their kids are either financially negligent or in serious denial. I say "handbag" here, but it could be any item where the money spent is out of line with the use you get out of it. Whether we're talking tickets to a hockey game or expensive clothing, we are all free to make our choices—but everything has a price.

The question is taboo, but as a society are we lacking in long-term "financial love" for our children? Can we deprive ourselves a little for their future happiness? Is it possible to cut $100 or $200 monthly from a budget item (the car, for instance) to achieve our savings goals? Not everyone has the luxury of making these choices, but we need to take the time to think about them.

Children can also contribute

If your child has been earning money from a part-time job from the age of sixteen or so, shouldn't you expect that he or she will contribute to an education fund? By contributing to an RESP, they will help to remove a big weight from their shoulders. It bears repeating: RESPs may be the most profitable investment there is, given the limited risk. It would be a shame not to take full advantage.

If you have children, you should consider an RESP even before you make contributions to a registered retirement savings plan or a tax-free savings account, as it's a great way to split income—as long as you and your kids see eye to eye.

The children are the ones who benefit from the RESP and who are taxed. The capital isn't taxable, unlike the returns the fund has accrued (interest, gains and grants, together called educational assistance payments), which are attributed to the children. So you could ask them to pay part of the family's expenses that you would have paid with your salary or returns from your personal portfolio.

So, before cutting the umbilical cord, before posting the first picture of the little one on Facebook, before unwrapping the first gift, the wise parent will open an RESP. It may not seem very exciting, but in the long term, does it ever pay off.

When my sister's son was born, I didn't buy him a teddy bear or spend $100 on an adorable outfit. I didn't pitch in for a diaper bin or a high-end stroller. No, **boring accountant that I am, I gave my nephew Théo a symbolic amount as an initial contribution to his RESP.**

Because a contribution to an RESP is like paying the phone bill: once you get into the habit, you forget what you are no longer spending that money on. The magic of automatic withdrawals from a bank account is that when that money isn't in your account, you are less likely to spend it.

Whether or not to keep it a secret

Should you tell your children that you are putting money aside every month for them? Opinions are divided. Will children make minimal efforts to save, or limit their personal contribution, because they know the fund will help finance their education, or is it an opportunity to teach them to dream big and aim high?

A colleague of mine had an interesting strategy with his daughter: he promised her he would "help her out" once she was at school. He didn't tell her how much his contribution would be, but it did relieve some of the pressure at the idea of having to foot a big bill down the road.

You can also use the capital in an RESP as a negotiating tool with children. For example, if children get their degree on time, you can give them part of the remaining capital toward a savings account.

FREE TIP!

To get children involved in investing, buy them stock in a company they are interested in (for example, Walt Disney or Caterpillar), provided the investment generates a good return and reflects your investor profile.

That way, you are tying the investment to something children are familiar with to get their attention, thereby introducing children to the wonderful world of investing through their RESPs.

Regardless of your strategy, when you have children, an RESP is a no-brainer.

Do you really need it?

Absolutely.

HOME OWNERSHIP
DO YOU REALLY NEED IT?

W hy is everyone so eager to own their own home? Maybe it's a nesting instinct or because a home is a symbol of both success and security. Owning a home may also fulfill the desire to decide for yourself where you want to live, and to make your place feel like it's your own.

No matter the reason, for many people being a homeowner confers a sense of accomplishment. People can't wait to post a selfie on Facebook showing them standing beside a Sold sign. You turn the key and you take possession. But financially speaking, is owning property an indispensable investment?

The real estate dream
The problem with real estate is that you hear about people who have made a fortune from it, but you never hear about the circumstances, luck or economic context that made that fortune possible.

One of the hot tips repeated in the many books on succeeding in real estate is to buy property at below market value. Really? I hadn't thought of that! Seriously, though, there's a lot of luck that factors into success in real estate investing, because there are so many economic and socio-demographic factors that are out of your control.

The right conditions

Let's take the example of those who bought income properties in Montreal just before the housing crisis of the early 2000s. The stars aligned for this generation. First, an apartment shortage pushed onto the market people who wanted decent housing without running the risk of having their rental unit taken back by the owner.

At the time, the price of real estate was rising because demand was growing faster than supply. Plus, with the technology stock bubble bursting, people were seeking to diversify their investments by putting more money into real estate.

Then, over a long period, interest rates dropped, and the more they dropped, the more buyers could borrow large amounts, and the more house prices increased. Before October 15, 2008, you could buy a house with a forty-year mortgage and *no* down payment.[1] It's no wonder the market exploded: we were letting people who were outright broke go deep into debt to buy a property. As a society, we so wanted Canadians to become homeowners that we didn't really pay attention to whether everyone could handle the responsibility in the long term.

RateHub.ca, a website that publishes data on competitive mortgage rates and credit card benefits in Canada, offered this curve of five-year, fixed-rate mortgages (these are the posted rates;

---

1   http://www.fin.gc.ca/no8/data/08-051_1-eng.asp

they're always higher than the negotiated rates, but the negotiated rate curve is based on the posted rates).[1]

Posted five-year fixed mortgage rates
1973 to present

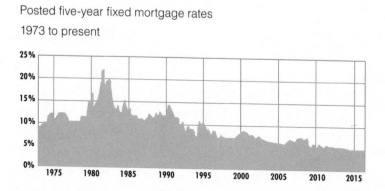

We can see that between 1981 and 2016, the rate gradually declined. A slight increase was offset by interventionist measures by the Bank of Canada after the credit crisis that sent shock waves around the world in 2008. The correction worked so well that lots of people made some very good deals in real estate. What's more, this graph shows how fundamentally different the lending scenario was in the 1980s and the beginning of the 1990s.

A reversal

Rapid gains convinced many investors that real estate was a sure way to make money. But that isn't always the case. Why not? It all depends on when you get into and out of a real estate cycle. Average long-term growth in the real estate market doesn't

---

1   https://www.ratehub.ca/5-year-fixed-mortgage-rate-history

necessarily generate spectacular gains when you include all the costs. People often forget to calculate the real costs when trying to demonstrate the profitability of any given investment.

In fact, current conditions as described below suggest that recent buyers are a long way from being assured of a significant profit in the short term.

Changes in lending conditions

Before Stephen Harper's former minister of finance Jim Flaherty left politics in 2014, he wanted to cool down the real estate market and overheated prices in Canada by reducing the amortization period for mortgages. In 2008, the federal government reduced the maximum amortization period for insured loans (with a down payment of at least 20 percent of the price of the property).

- ✔ The maximum amortization period for a mortgage dropped from forty to twenty-five years.
- ✔ The minimum down payment on houses over $50,000 was increased.
- ✔ Mortgages can no longer be insured for a building worth $1,000,000 or more.

These measures caused some people to put off buying a single-family dwelling and others to look to different types of affordable housing.

A condo explosion

In recent years, condo construction projects have flooded the market with new units. At one point in 2016 the price of condos was considered too high in the Quebec City area. In June 2016, it was announced that the price of condos had dropped 5 percent in Quebec City because of excess supply.[1]

By as early as December 2015, the number of unsold new condos in Montreal was approaching 2,500 units.[2] Today, there are fears that the real estate market will become overheated in the Vancouver and Toronto areas.[3] This data shows that investors who are thinking of making big money in real estate are looking at the sector through rose-coloured glasses.

High debt ratios

While it appears to be levelling off, the personal debt ratio was 170.4 percent at the end of 2017 (household debt/disposable income).[4] Obviously, this ratio includes mortgages.

It makes sense that your debt ratio is high when you're young; in theory, over time, repaying the principal reduces the debt ratio. But a ratio of 170.4 percent is very high, limiting the ability of households to borrow more to pay a high price for somewhere to live.

---

1   www.journaldequebec.com/2016/06/06/les-prix-des-condos-en-baisse-de-5-a-quebec

2   affaires.lapresse.ca/economie/immobilier/201604/27/01-4975596-immobiliersurevaluation-elevee-a-quebec-et-moderee-a-montreal.php

3   affaires.lapresse.ca/opinions/chroniques/rudy-le-cours/201606/10/01-4990396-lendettement-des-menages-fragilise-leconomie.php

4   http://www.cbc.ca/news/business/statistics-canada-debt-data-1.4577306

High consumer debt

Canadians' consumer debt was \$22,837 in the fourth quarter of 2017.[1] This rising personal debt limits many people's ability to invest in a home or an income property.

Vacancy rate

In December 2015, the Canada Mortgage and Housing Corporation forecast that in 2017 the vacancy rate for rental buildings in the metropolitan area of Montreal would be 4.4 percent. In theory, a rate of around 3 percent is considered to be balanced.[2] So when someone has the choice between buying or renting, the availability of housing can influence their decision and affect demand for property.

These are just a few factors that explain a reality. In the next fifteen years, real estate investors can't expect the same glory days that their counterparts enjoyed over the past fifteen years. And don't forget that baby boomers will start dying off in large numbers in the coming decades (cold-hearted, I know); the demographic curve will influence the housing stock.

It's why promoting immigration makes good sense: it will help us maintain the value of homes and address weaknesses in our demographic growth. So yes, personal finance can also be political.

---

1   https://www.consumer.equifax.ca/fr/au-sujet-d-equifax/bulletins-de-presse/-/blogs/total-canadian-consumer-debt-climbs-to-over-1-8-trillion-but-delinquencies-and-bankruptcies-edge-down/

2   affaires.lapresse.ca/economie/immobilier/201512/03/01-4927375-immobilier-signesde-surevaluation-eleves-a-montreal.php

Forced savings

You often hear that investing in real estate is a way of forcing yourself to save. It's true that for some people the only way to invest is to make a mortgage payment. But that doesn't mean that it's the best method of saving that will yield the best returns.

Homeowners do, however, enjoy one tremendous tax advantage: the capital gain on your primary residence isn't taxed for as long as you own the property. Still, this advantage on its own doesn't justify concentrating all your risk in the real estate sector and thinking of your home as your retirement plan.

Say you turn sixty-five and the "retirement plan" you live in is actually a place that is a reasonable size and affordable. You're not necessarily going to feel like selling and moving somewhere else. After all, you have to live somewhere. Your house doesn't give you a cheque to pay for groceries. But if that's been your whole retirement plan, you'd have to sell it and find somewhere else to live, so you would end up paying rent. Back to square one!

Owning a house is not a proper retirement plan or a way to deal with life's little hiccups. My grandparents never left their final home. Neither did my parents, and I hope to follow in their footsteps. My goal is to avoid being put in an elder-care warehouse, waiting to be served mystery meat and instant mashed potatoes.

Money out the window

Plenty of people think that paying rent is throwing money out the window. This argument is again the result of an incomplete analysis and has an inherent, unwitting bias. Tenants pay rent, which gives them the freedom to leave their apartment at the end of the lease. They don't take the financial risk of owning a place, and they don't have to pay someone to maintain the property.

Basically, tenants are being provided a service by owners; they pay to be provided with housing in good condition for a price set in advance. **To say that paying rent is throwing money out the window is an oversimplification.** Living somewhere costs money, full stop. It doesn't matter whether or not you own the place where you live.

Let's take the example of a duplex in Montreal. Let's say that the tenant occupies 40 percent of the living space. If the owner pays property and school taxes of $5,800, that means that theoretically the tenant has $2,320 in taxes included in the cost of the apartment. As well, to buy an equivalent dwelling, he or she would have to pay interest on the loan.

Discipline

When you buy a condo, you have to budget hundreds of dollars per month in condo fees for shared expenses and a contingency fund. So, again, living somewhere costs money; it's not just an investment. But if you were paying only rent, you'd be subcontracting the risk of the investment.

Tenants often don't have the discipline to save the difference between the amount they would pay if they owned a condo and the cost of rent. But if people set up automatic withdrawals in an amount equal to this difference for long-term investing, they would be surprised at how the return could match the return on a condo over time.

Take the example of the homeowner who says, "I made $100,000 on my house in fifteen years." That works out to a 2.8 percent return compounded annually on a $200,000 investment.

This calculation doesn't include renovations, ongoing costs and maintenance.

That said, the $100,000 profit on a primary residence generally isn't taxable. We should also note that the calculation does not take into account the value of money over time. The $200,000 from 2001 doesn't have the same value as $200,000 in 2016.

Fixed or variable rate?

I don't know how many times I've been asked this question lately. If there were an easy, one-size-fits-all answer, you'd automatically choose the more competitive of the two rates. But things are actually more nuanced than that and depend on the investor's circumstances and profile.

A variable rate (particularly negotiated) is generally more competitive than a fixed rate, but it involves a level of uncertainty. So rather than repeating what I've said countless times, I will quote Gérald Fillion's blog.[1]

"In a book François Delorme and I published in 2014,[2] we referred to advice from the site canadianmortgagetrends.com on this matter. Before choosing a fixed or variable rate, you need to ask yourself five questions:

1. Is your income stable?
2. Is your level of debt sustainable?
3. Can you refinance your mortgage based on the value of your house?

---

1   blogues.radio-canada.ca/geraldfillion/2015/08/21/alors-taux-fixe-ou-taux-variable

2   Gérard Fillion and François Delorme, *Vos questions sur l'économie*, Montréal, Éditions La Presse, 2014.

4. If you fall on hard times, do you have the cash on hand to pay your mortgage for six months?

5. A 2.5 percent bump in interest rates can increase your payments by 30 percent. Were you aware of that?

Depending on how you answer these questions, you will know whether you can live with a variable rate or will sleep better with a fixed rate. Historically, you pay less interest with a variable rate. But a fixed rate is more popular."[1]

At the end of the day, you need to understand that even if a variable rate increases over a five-year period and is higher than the fixed rate that was negotiated at the beginning of the term, you can still come out ahead. If you have a variable rate that is much lower than the fixed rate for the first two or three years, it can make up for a higher rate the two following years.

Why? Because the interest rate in the first few years is calculated on a larger balance of the principal. We should also note that financial institutions like five-year fixed rates, which is why they like selling five-year terms.

Why become a homeowner?

You'll notice that sellers who talk up their real estate success never mention the people who lost their shirts. When investing in real estate, certain conditions make for success, and they're not necessarily present at the moment you want to invest.

When choosing a place to live, you need to consider your ability to pay (once your other financial obligations are met) and not just possible gains based on speculation.

---

1 blogues.radio-canada.ca/geraldfillion/2015/08/21/alors-taux-fixe-ou-taux-variable

Is your property an investment? Perhaps, if you were lucky enough to buy in favourable conditions, something you can only know for certain in hindsight. Regardless, what counts in investing is diversification. Are you diversified? Or are you taking a risk by putting all your eggs into one type of investment basket?

Owning a home: do you really need it? No. The important thing is to invest. Real estate isn't the only investment option.

CHILDREN
DO YOU REALLY NEED THEM?

T he subject of this chapter could definitely rub some people the wrong way. They'll say that life isn't all about accounting and economics.

And I agree. But only to a point: for decades our society has been structured economically to promote particular family structures and discourage others.

In this chapter I encourage you to think about how personal choices (for example, deciding whether or not to have children, and how many) are subject to the economic realities of the world we live in. I'm in no way passing judgment—I'm just analyzing the family and the number of people in it from an economic standpoint.

To have or not to have children?

Having children can be an altruistic gesture, because all of a sudden a large part of our time is devoted to a little person for whom we will endure a lot of self-denial.

We put ourselves second for the first time in our lives, and we make decisions based on what's best for the little one. We don't even listen to our bodies anymore, because the little angel is calling the shots, day and night. And that's just the way it's going to be for a few years.

But the urge to reproduce is also a bit selfish. We dream of our legacy continuing. We want an extension of ourselves. We want to lend meaning to our lives.

I know people who have never had children, by choice or bad luck. Others, thanks to multiple births, had more than they planned for. You don't necessarily have complete control over how many children you have. You may want a family with two kids, but Mother Nature may have other ideas, whether as an "oops" with birth control or a twist of fate.

Contrary to conventional wisdom, not having children has its upside. Without the responsibility of children, you retain your freedom, and your life belongs to you. Your relationship with your partner won't risk being worn down by the daily grind of child care. You can be casual and disorganized; you can live in a smaller space, be impulsive and spontaneous, and follow your bliss, whatever you decide that to be.

Truly, there are two sides of the family coin: with or without children. Our society seems to value only one model: reproduction. When parents judge couples who don't have kids, could it actually be that they're a little envious?

Marketing and the family of four

When it comes to family, our society has developed what is called a "preferred habitat." If you are going to start a family, the four-person family is the model. Since the beginning of the 1980s, two or fewer offspring has been the norm for families with children.[1] The economic world took heed, and commercial offerings gradually adapted to the family of four. For example:

✔ Many establishments offer family passes for two adults and two children.
✔ Swiss Chalet's Family Pack comes with four rolls and four single sides. (Apparently nature got it right by giving chickens two legs and two breasts.)
✔ A common hotel room configuration features two queen-size beds, perfect for two parents and two kids.
✔ Children under two can fly free if they sit on an adult's lap: limit of two children per family.

The same principle applies when you buy a car: a compact, subcompact or sedan can comfortably seat four people. We often forget that, in another era, six could sit comfortably in a sedan, with a long front seat that accommodated three people. Then cars slowly shifted from six seats to four, adapting to the smaller family size.

Housing favours small families

The housing supply doesn't meet the needs of large families. Speaking strictly economically, it's hard to justify building large dwellings with more than three bedrooms.

Why? First, while demand exists at a certain price, developers prefer to build smaller units. They turn more of a profit selling smaller places than larger ones because price is not proportional

1   www.mfa.gouv.qc.ca/fr/publication/documents/sf_portrait_stat_complet_11.pdf, p. 145

to the number of rooms. Large families just aren't the target market for series construction.

As a general rule, the more units you can sell for a given-size lot, the more developers are interested. From a purely economic point of view, landlords who have apartments to rent prefer to rent five small ones rather than three large ones, because this increases rental income and spreads out the risk of non-payment. As a result, large families have more limited supply to choose from in rental housing. The larger the family, the greater the constraints, and the harder the search. Of course, there is demand for large apartments, but, ironically, the fewer children you have, the more you are able to afford such accommodations.

The risk of parental separation

Why talk about this, when everything was going so well? Because having children and hoping to stay a united family until they are fully vaccinated, over eighteen and living on their own is wildly optimistic.

The odds are not in couples' favour. Too many factors exist that can damage relationships: children, personal frustrations, work, routine, bills to pay, and on and on. Whatever the reason, separation is often the only option.

Even when both people in a relationship manage to control their impulses and ensure their own personal well-being, no one is immune to circumstances that are beyond their control. Will she leave you for a co-worker? Will a chronic illness or premature death strike? Strong headwinds can eventually sink the relationship boat.

Bravo for the survivors, but people need to be aware that, from the beginning, the odds are not on the side of couples. Often, the lover of today becomes, in the words of both Elliott Smith and Gotye, the "somebody that I used to know" of tomorrow.

The blended family: easier for small families

Being a single parent of young children is in itself financially difficult. First, you may need to find a new place to live. Plus, you no longer benefit from the economies of scale couples enjoy, because you have to pay a series of major fixed expenses on your own.

Once the nuclear family falls apart, sometimes the ex-spouse goes on to meet someone in a similar situation and eventually attempts to form a blended family. Then there will be all kinds of extra things to manage: the kids' schedules, schools, sports, vacation, and finding housing ample enough for everyone. Basically, it can be hard to make it work, so you have to be prepared to survive as a single parent, at least for a while.

Another child?

I'll just come out and say it: the world doesn't need another human being. And with the billions of people we already have, some parts of the planet could definitely use a break in, or need to put the brakes on, the number of births.

So why bring more than two children into the world? Because family is wonderful? It's true, it's wonderful. The togetherness, the family gatherings—all those Norman Rockwell–type images.

But large families are an anomaly in today's world; they are a counter-current in an era where risks are greater. However much you try to keep it simple, with two working parents, bills to pay, homework, baths, meals, activities, and so on, life starts to resemble one long series of endlessly repeating tasks, like Sisyphus with his rock.

The number of children we have depends on our ability to put money aside for their education, to feed them, to take them on vacation, and so on. Each additional child hampers the couple's ability to allocate financial resources to all the others.

True, there are economies of scale in larger families. But while you may be able to hand down a pair of pants from an older to a younger brother, you can't hand down a degree. Your love for your children may be limitless, but your resources are not.

From a particular perspective, one way of looking at a child is to consider the long list of bills you'll need to pay for eighteen years:

- ✔ Cloth diapers or disposable: they both stink.
- ✔ Clothes: always too small or too beat up.
- ✔ Toys and USOs (Unidentified Scattered Objects).
- ✔ Bikes: the second child's is never new.
- ✔ Meals: three a day, and a fourth that starts in adolescence.
- ✔ Private school: because your child is worth more than the others (#sarcasm).
- ✔ Cellphones: a source of social validation.
- ✔ Classes, sports, activities: all the things parents never did and are experiencing vicariously through their children.
- ✔ An apartment in another city: when your child is born in Montreal but wants to study marine biology in Vancouver.
- ✔ Clothes that are on trend: because you don't want your kid to be rejected.
- ✔ The list never ends.

Are you a bit stunned after finishing this chapter? It's hard to accurately assess the cost of having children, because it all depends on the life you offer them. Cloth diapers? Used clothes? Private school? It's worth thinking ahead about how much each decision will cost.

So—children, do you really need them? You know what's in your heart and your wallet. No, it's not just a matter of money, but everything in life has a price. This is why asking, "One child—or two, or three, or four or more—do you really need it?" makes sense.

PERSONAL INSURANCE
DO YOU REALLY NEED IT?

P eople like to buy lottery tickets. The ridiculous idea that manna could fall from heaven and change our lives in an instant is exciting. But those same people also don't like spending for an uncertain benefit. This shows the bipolar nature of so many of us when it comes to insurance: we either over-insure or dangerously under-insure.

According to my colleagues at the CEGEP Régional de Lanaudière in L'Assomption who work in the area, it is harder to convince people to take out insurance than to convince them not to. Similarly, it is easier to convince people to buy a new car than to plan for replacing a roof. Human nature often has little to do with logic.

Insurance should protect you against a risk you can't afford to take. Nothing more. It's not to fuel fantasies of passing Go and collecting $100,000. Or thinking that bad things happen only to other people. In other words, you have to ask yourself whether, in the event of a tragedy, such as death, illness, disability or an accident, you will be able to foot the bill. You take out insurance to be able to pay that bill, not to be able to say, "See ya, boss!"

Let's use clothing as an illustration. When you bring a change of clothes with you when you go out, just in case something happens, you don't buy a mobile walk-in closet filled with evening wear towed by a Tesla. You just want to cover the reasonable risk. You're not trying to end up in a better position after the incident you were protecting yourself from. Similarly, you don't go camping for three weeks with just a T-shirt and a pair of shorts.

Covering a risk

This argument points to an important fact: if you were sure you would live to be eighty, you wouldn't take out life insurance; instead, you would invest the money to have enough to provide for your own well-being and that of your loved ones. You need to use common sense. Insurers are after profit. They accumulate premiums paid, invest them, and pay benefits with the capital and profits earned.

The advantage the insurer has over the individual is the ability to distribute risk among many people. They may lose money on Mario's early demise, but Jacqueline will have paid for life insurance her entire life up to age ninety-five, and the death benefit will be lower than the capital and returns generated by the premiums. So it is premature death that you are looking to cover when you take out life insurance.

When you die at age eighty, life insurance is an investment with a fairly clear return. I pay a premium for sixty years, at the end of which I get a portion of the capital and the returns back. The higher the benefit, the more insurance premiums will sap cash from your life today against a greater future benefit.

If you want $1 million in insurance coverage, but you're the type who pays for coffee every morning with your line of credit, you are being inconsistent. Along the same line of thinking, children's educations are financed over the course of seventeen years, not sixty. What is the point of taking insurance to pay for an education until your children are pre-retirement age?

You need an insurance cocktail that reflects your needs and not expensive insurance that covers everything until you die.

Before, during and after children

The life of an insured person can be summed up in three phases: before, during and after children. This may seem simplistic, but these are three periods with very distinct needs.

1. Before children: When you are single and childless, the goal of personal insurance is to maintain your insurability. Otherwise, why pay in when you don't have anybody in your life to mourn your untimely demise?

    Why maintain your insurability? Have you ever answered an insurance company questionnaire? Each question targets a risk factor and can increase premiums. Pretty soon they will consider the use of Tinder and Snapchat as risk factors as serious as smoking.

    The older you are, the greater the risk of having an illness or a chronic condition that will affect your ability to get insurance or work. It's not easy to get insurance at age thirty-five when you've had three bouts of cancer, or when a disease lands you in a wheelchair and you have to turn to crowdfunding to pay for a caregiver to bathe you. These things can happen to anyone.

2.   During children: As long as you have children under your care, you have a major responsibility. You need to provide for them. Whether you're dead or alive, you shouldn't leave them in poverty out of negligence. The goal is to have enough insurance to "carry them to term," sort of like an eighteen-plus-year pregnancy.

3.   After children: Once the house is paid off, you are saving systematically and you have planned for your retirement, your relationship with insurance changes. Worst-case scenario, you die earlier than expected, and your savings will go to the surviving spouse and the children. This is the point when life insurance takes a back seat.

   Time has elapsed, so you have reduced the risk related to the period of time you would have been unable to work. For instance, is it riskier not to be insured, knowing you could die at age twenty-five leaving two children behind, or to not have life insurance at age sixty with two independent children and the house paid for?

The moral of the story is that your needs change depending on your stage of life. Like anything else, insurance needs can be temporary.

Life insurance, not lotto insurance

When people meet an insurance broker to take out whole or universal (valid until death) life insurance, why do they get carried away with the amount of coverage?

"If you die, how much money do you think your spouse would need to pick up the pieces?"

"Well, she'd have to pay the mortgage and the bills, raise the children, pay for their education . . . I think $1 million in coverage isn't overreaching. Plus, she will have to get over my death, which won't be easy." (In my case, I think my spouse would pop open the champagne.)

The broker's job is to advise you and meet your needs. So you need to express those needs clearly. First of all, you shouldn't overestimate how long the surviving spouse won't be working. Sometimes getting back to work after a loss offers new perspective. If a broker suggests that your spouse would spend a year not working, you need to keep things in perspective. Who knows? Maybe the surviving spouse will soon find happiness with someone else.

Second, why carry life insurance until age eighty to cover a risk that will no longer exist at that point? Let's take the example of mortgage payments. Let's say a couple owns a new home with a 25-year mortgage. Why not take out temporary life insurance for that period? The advantage of temporary life insurance is the cost of the premium, which is much lower, because the insurer pays out nothing if the insured person does not die prematurely.

Let's look at the logic of this. When you sign for a mortgage, your banker generally wants to sell you life and disability insurance on the loan. You need to figure out whether you already have insurance to cover that risk.

You need to understand what's in bank advisers' interests. They have performance targets. They have to reach their annual sales volume. A $300,000 mortgage gets them partway to meeting their loan volume goal. If advisers sell you insurance, they have doubled their volume in a single transaction. Their volume will be $300,000 for the mortgage and $300,000 for the insurance.

But is your financial institution's mortgage insurance in your best interests? The answer is often no. A mortgage balance goes down. In this example, at the end of twenty-five years, it's $0. So why pay for life insurance at a non-negligible monthly cost if your coverage is dropping? For example, say you pay insurance premiums for twenty-four years, and your spouse dies. Great. You'll receive a paltry amount because virtually the entire principal has been repaid.

In fact, you would be covered for the residual value of the mortgage, let's say less than $10,000, when with temporary life insurance you would be covered for a fixed amount equal to the initial loan, in other words $300,000. Yet you would have paid a considerable amount over the twenty-four years.

This is why temporary life insurance makes sense: the cost is low, and the amount of coverage doesn't drop over time. However, a private insurer can also offer you protection on a fixed or diminishing amount. You need to understand the product before taking it.

If you change financial institutions, will your insurance follow you? If you renew your mortgage with a different financial institution, you need to ask what will happen to your insurance.

Before listening to your adviser, take a few minutes to think about it.

Disability insurance: the forgotten child

Disability insurance is what you really need (remember the example of bath crowdfunding). The older you are, the more expensive this insurance is monthly. But I think it's essential. For obvious reasons, I hope I never have to use it!

If you are a salaried employee, you probably have disability insurance. **But if you are self-employed and you don't have disability insurance in your portfolio, drop everything you're doing and call a professional!** When you're disabled, you aren't dead. It will be the people closest to you who'll pay the price for your financial irresponsibility should you become disabled, and it will cost you too.

No one is immune to disability. A car accident, a bike accident, a bad fall or a major health problem happens in the blink of an eye. That's why it is risky to be self-employed without disability insurance. Is it really worth it?

Critical illness insurance

I don't have critical illness insurance. My broker tried to sell me some a few years ago. Ironically, he has since died of a critical illness. I didn't want the insurance at the time. I already had life insurance and disability insurance, which was costing me $100 a month for minimal coverage.

As the name suggests, critical illness insurance provides coverage in the event of a serious illness. For example, if you get cancer and need to be hospitalized, you will receive a cheque. Obviously, many people think this insurance is necessary because of the risk of serious illness. It's true, but at some point you also have your assets and savings to fall back on. So, if you get terminal cancer and the doctors have given you six months, there is nothing to stop you from dipping into your RRSPs to pay the bills.

This is a personal decision, based on your financial health and the risk you're able to take. The earlier you invest, the more assets you have, and the greater your leeway not to take out insurance for certain obligations.

The most serious illness you need to insure yourself against is the frivolousness of failing to plan. Some people vaccinate themselves against it, while others leave themselves vulnerable to whatever virus is carried on the air.

Basically, you always have to keep an important question in mind: do I really need this coverage? Will I end up homeless or in a tight spot without it? If the answer is no, why take it? Would you wear a helmet to go for a walk or a wetsuit to take a shower? No, because you don't really need them. So why carry too much insurance?

FREE TIP!

Before going to the grocery store, we check what's already in the fridge. But when it comes to insurance, we often start off thinking we have no foundation. Before you shop for insurance, look at what your employer offers. For instance, your insurance may pay out a year's salary in the event of your death.

Also, ask yourself about your loyalty to employers. If your CV has a job for every year you've worked, it would be as risky to bank on stability as a hockey player hitting the ice with skate guards on.

Life insurance on your children. Really?

When children are born, we mistakenly make a connection between our love for them and the need to insure them. The common sales pitch is that insuring a child for $50,000 costs just a few dollars a month.

But why insure a child? After all, a child's death frees up tens of thousands of dollars, because you have fewer expenses: clothing, activities, food, child care, spending money, family vacations, sports equipment, and so on. So from a purely economic point of view, a child's death means more cash flow.

As you read these lines, your love for your children got the better of your common sense, and you may be thinking this McSween guy has no heart. But if you read dispassionately, you will see that the greatest economic risks associated with a child's death are the funeral expenses and the parents' inability to work. (If that should come to pass, perhaps your employer has a policy for granting a certain leave of absence.)

The only viable economic argument for insuring children is to maintain their insurability. If certain things happen—for instance, being diagnosed with cancer at fifteen—it can be hard to get reasonably priced insurance. Having paid into life insurance for a child since birth allows you to pass the insurance on once the child is an adult.

Therefore, you need to think about the consequences of putting off insurance. You definitely need to start thinking seriously about it in your early twenties. Once you have a family, you will probably appreciate the fact that you paid into life insurance early on. The longer you wait to insure yourself, the higher the monthly premium, and the greater the risk that you won't be able to get insurance.

FREE TIP!

A rider can be added to the parents' life insurance for a low annual amount to cover the funeral costs for an existing or future child.[1] You can also change this coverage into permanent insurance later on.

What about critical illness insurance for my children?

After life insurance, some advisers or brokers recommend critical illness insurance with premium refunds for children. If a child gets sick and has to be hospitalized for an extended period, the parents' disability insurance through their employer is no help.

If a child gets seriously ill, one of the parents might have to quit work. The financial difficulties that could result are easy to imagine. I don't have critical illness insurance for my children as this book goes to print, but I'm considering it. You just have to look at parents turning to social media for help to understand the financial consequences of not having this sort of coverage.

Vision and dental care

Does your employer offer optional dental insurance and vision care? Have you considered not contributing to the plan and paying your annual dental expenses yourself? If your group insurance reimburses you for annual cleaning, is it possible that you are paying for it in one way or another?

Obviously, if you lose half your teeth playing street hockey, that's another story. The real question is whether it is worth it to

---

1   A rider is an add-on provision to a basic insurance policy that provides additional benefits to the policyholder at a cost. Source: http://www.investopedia.com/terms/r/rider.asp

insure yourself so much for these services. It's a personal question that only you can answer.

Insuring taxes?

As you look for insurance, someone may try to sell you insurance to cover any taxes owing upon your death. The question is, why do you need this coverage? What risk are you trying to insure against? The risk of paying taxes? Really? That said, certain situations could make it worthwhile.

For example, a couple wants to pass on their bucolic slice of the countryside to their children. The problem is that the lot is so big that capital gains will be taxed (the land exceeds the limit for a primary residence). Will there be enough cash to save the family estate while paying the fair share of taxes due upon the death? If the answer is yes, why take out insurance for the tax bill?

Let's also take the example of an income property that has gained a great deal in value over the years and is handed down in a buyers' market. Life insurance could pay the taxes on the capital gains and prevent the estate from having to sell the building at a reduced price to pay the tax bill.

Ask yourself what the goal of the insurance is. If your heirs aren't at risk, why insure them?

The role of brokers and advisers

The role of insurance brokers or advisers is to answer the customer's questions—nothing more, nothing less. So while they obviously want to get the best return possible, they know that customers will be satisfied only if they are properly served in the short, medium and long term.

Often, customers take out too little or too much insurance because they give advisers the wrong message. For their part, advisers have to be sure they properly identify the customers' needs and know what they can afford. I know there are prejudices out there about insurance advisers and brokers. But having spent a lot of time with them during my teaching career, I can tell you that they are like accountants—it pays to get to know them.

> Cover your ass, and only your own. Cover it when it is most at risk, but don't cover any more than your ass. And if you don't, you may find it in a sling.

NB: Again, this chapter is not meant to be exhaustive training on insurance. It is just a wake-up call for people who are under-insured. If, as you read it, you started to have some panicky feelings, maybe it's time to call an insurance broker or adviser.

PROPERTY AND CASUALTY INSURANCE
DO YOU REALLY NEED IT?

When we buy new stuff (see "New Stuff: Do You Really Need It?" on page 152), we tend to take out excessive insurance on it at a prohibitive cost. But do we really need to insure it? Do we really need insurance coverage for any and every possible damage?

Extended warrantie$

Let's take the example of extended warranties. They are, in essence, a form of insurance. Sometimes they are called maintenance plans.

We can argue about the term, like Quebec premier Philippe Couillard trying to decide between "austerity" and "a strict budget." But the principle is still about shelling out a certain amount right now to protect yourself against possible future damage or a potential accident.

What do you think salespeople do after selling an extended warranty on a product? They wash their hands. Why? Because they feel dirty, or like Pontius Pilate. You negotiated the price of your amp effectively, but in just five minutes, right before finalizing the transaction, the salesperson pulls another 30 percent (let's say) of the value of your purchase out of you to insure the product against breakage for five years. That's why salespeople don't feel clean.

Isn't it ironic to hear about the high quality of a product for twenty minutes and then be told it could break? Or that you may have bought a lemon? Soon they will be trying to sell extended warranties on tombstones. Possible slogans: "Our tombstones carry a lifetime warranty" or "Peace-of-mind insurance for the great beyond."

Instead, you should be asking yourself whether, in the event the object in question breaks in the first few years, you'll have the money to replace it. If the answer is no, it's because you don't have the money to buy it. **Don't forget that the point of insurance is to protect yourself against any risk that is too great.** It is unlikely that a number of valuable objects will give up the ghost at the same time, unless there is a fire or you are robbed.

The flawed logic of the cost of extended warranties is even funnier when you add up the price of purchases. Imagine that you have three products that cost $1,000 each. The salesperson offers you an extended warranty that costs $300 for each of the products. That totals $900 in warranties for $3,000 in purchases.

Rather than paying for the warranties, why not invest the $900 in a TFSA? You would have to be pretty unlucky to need to replace all three things in a short time frame. If nothing breaks, you will have saved $900. If all three things break at once, run out and buy a lottery ticket. **The best strategy is always to decline the extended warranty.**

Let's apply this logic to all household items and imagine the total saved by declining extended warranties. Given the savings, shelling out from time to time to replace something is the lesser of two evils.

When you think about it, paying 30 percent in insurance to enable you to buy an equivalent piece of equipment within five years is pretty ridiculous. The price of the insurance is high, particularly since, chances are, customers will never make a claim.

Salespeople's modus operandi is to mention the extended warranty just when you are ready to pay. So get your credit card out and get ready to say, "No, thank you." Just like you do for the Lotto Max Extra.

"Free" warranties

Before asking yourself whether you need an extended warranty (or maintenance plan), you need to ask yourself what warranties you have already paid for.

For example, when you pay for something by credit card, the issuing company sometimes doubles the length of the manufacturer's warranty, up to a certain limit. If the warranty is twelve months, paying with a credit card can extend the warranty to twenty-four months.

You are also protected by the legal warranty, which is the automatic, minimum consumer protection set by law. Before making any purchase, especially a high-cost item, be sure to check the specific terms of the warranty.

THE MAPLE SYRUP RANGE HOOD

My friend bought a retractable range hood (it looks fantastic). One day, he decided to make maple syrup at home. He boiled the maple sap on his stove.

After an hour, the hood stopped working (obviously—the sugar had completely crystallized the mechanism). He called the salesperson (not mentioning that he had had the brilliant idea of boiling maple sap for an hour, two inches away from the range hood).

Salesperson: Hello, Salesperson here. How can I help you?

Friend: My range hood isn't working anymore. Can you send someone to take a look?

(I'll skip the part of the conversation in which my friend identifies himself, proves that he bought the range hood, and so on.)

Salesperson: I see that you bought it thirteen months ago, so I'm afraid the one-year warranty no longer applies.

Friend: You mean that I paid $1,200 for a range hood that's broken?

Salesperson: You didn't take the maintenance plan.

Friend: Do you really want me to tell you about the legal warranty? Do you really want us to spend time in small claims court, wasting your time, and mine, to have a judge read you the letter of the law? Because I should mention, I have lots of time to go to small claims court, because I'm a CEGEP teacher.

Salesperson: I'll send someone right away.

The moral of the story? You are already paying for a legal warranty. Why not use it to negotiate what you want?

Home insurance

When you insure your home, don't forget that the things in the house are older and depreciated, and to replace them you'll have to buy new possessions at today's prices; you don't have time to shop for sales when everything has gone up in smoke.

This raises the issue of under-insurance: when people with insurance aren't covered for the right amount, they can leave serious money on the table because they were too cheap to pay the actual price of appropriate coverage every month. After a disaster, it's not easy to find the hundreds of dollars needed to replace the shoes we owned.

If you are a tenant, home insurance doesn't cost as much as you think. But be careful: you shouldn't limit your coverage to your property; you also need insurance for bodily harm and damage caused to other people's property. Basically, you need a minimum of personal liability insurance (or, in Quebec, civil liability insurance).

 As an example, home insurance has to cover you if you accidentally set fire to the triplex you live in. A neighbour is killed in the fire, the triplex is a total loss, and fire and water damage the building next door.

If you have the right coverage, what happens if you change how your dwelling is used? For example, you may sublet your place to pay for a trip. This gets you into a different level of risk than that declared to your insurer.

Airbnb: handle with care!

Imagine the following scenario: you rent your house or apartment on Airbnb or another sharing economy site or app. You "forget" to declare the income on your taxes, you don't notify your landlord if you have one, and it would never occur to you to call your insurer.

- ✔ What happens if a short-term tenant accidentally sets fire to the house?
- ✔ What happens if a washing machine overflows and causes damage?
- ✔ What happens if a disaster not caused by the tenant occurs while the place is rented?

You need to talk to your insurer and make sure that, in the event of something bad happening, your insurance policy doesn't have as many holes as a strainer.

Subletting your home increases the risk for the insurer. It would definitely charge an additional premium if it knew how the inhabited space is being used. In the event of an accident, an insurer who was not notified could well wash its hands.

Do you use Airbnb insurance? Beware of potential problems. If you find yourself in a situation mentioned in an exclusion on your contract, what would you do if your insurance company refused to cover you?

Car insurance: keep a cool head

We're going to nip the first myth in the bud: dealing with an insurance broker doesn't necessarily mean getting the best price. No insurer or broker can claim to offer the best price all the time. Making a few phone calls yourself could save you a considerable amount.

For example, I had a 34-year-old friend who dealt with an insurance broker for his car. The best price the broker gave him was more than $1,000 per year. A simple call to a competitor got him the same coverage for under $700.

Why? Because insurers choose their "preferred habitats"; that is, they target a specific clientele. If your profile doesn't fall within certain criteria, they will agree to cover you, but at a premium.

An important point to consider when you are shopping for car insurance is the type of car that needs to be insured. Before buying a car, it's worthwhile to call your insurer to understand the impact your choice will have on monthly payments.

Plus, certain models of car cost more to repair or are more in demand among thieves for parts. Before shopping for a car, it is a good idea to research these details, because they'll factor into the cost of maintenance, repairs and insurance.

You may be surprised at the cost of insuring a new economical car; in the case of accident, will it be more easily written off than a more high-end vehicle? Instinct can be your worst enemy when it comes to insurance.

FREE TIP!

Do you need to insure your clunker against damage? The answer is no. If you have a major accident with a car worth less than $1,500 (for example, a 1992 Ford Tempo with fuzzy seat covers), it won't be worth anything, so why insure it? This is when you get one-way insurance, i.e., for damages caused to the other accident victim.

Most insurers don't offer two-way insurance once the vehicle has reached a certain age. Insuring a vehicle against damage after ten years may not make sense. It needs to be looked at case by case.

Insure the creditor

You need to keep in mind that insurance may be required by people or institutions with a financial stake in a property, for example, a mortgage lender, a car lender or a landlord. Insurance is not limited to the interests of the property owner, but to any physical or moral person with a financial interest in that property.

Replacement value insurance

The "replacement value" clause in an insurance contract is a mystery to me. I think it is the most useless insurance protection there is.

When you use a car, you wear it out. Whether or not you use the car, it depreciates quickly, with a capital Q. Insuring for replacement value basically means wanting to maintain the original value of your vehicle.

If you drive a 2018 Civic and you have an accident in 2019, you want to be able to replace your 2018 Civic with a new vehicle. But this comes at a price: you will pay to maintain the value of a car that automatically loses value once it is bought.

This makes about as much sense as going to McDonald's for a healthy meal or getting tips on humility from Kanye West. That said, replacement value insurance can allow you to use original quality parts in the case of a partial loss.

There is one case in which you may think replacement value coverage is useful: insuring the difference between the amount owing on the vehicle and its value. Logically, replacement value is worth it only during the first two or three years of ownership. This is the period when the drop in the vehicle's value is likely to be significantly higher than the amount paid off the loan. But before opting for replacement value, you need to think about the risk you are trying to cover. Are you playing the lottery or are you protecting yourself in case of misfortune?

Insurance against online identity theft

The more you use the Internet, the more you end up trusting it. It becomes a friend; you tell it everything. Are you covered for identity theft? No. Should you be? Maybe.

Is it a risk you can't deal with? That depends on the fraud you are a victim of. You can take all reasonable measures on your end, but if a company inadvertently discloses your private information online, what do you do then? Some insurers offer free assistance in cases of identity theft, but we're talking about assistance, not coverage.

Identity theft insurance, which covers costs associated with this type of theft (up to a maximum), is available. It is not on my list of priorities, but it exists. It's like an Avril Lavigne CD on sale in a bin at the drugstore; you're an adult, you can buy it, but will you listen to it?

So how do you make sure you are properly insured?

You shouldn't insure yourself for everything and end up eating KD every day. In an ideal world, people would understand an insurance contract when they read it, but then some people get lost in the shopping mall. Taking a few hours and seeking out the right type of advice is a good idea.

We keep coming back to the same idea: the more things you have, the more you have to maintain them, and the more their maintenance and replacement costs end up eating away at a family's discretionary spending.

Insuring things: do you really need to? It depends on the thing itself and the amount you have to pay.

NB: This chapter is incomplete. I could write three volumes on insurance alone. My goal here is just to make readers think about the cost of insurance and what it covers. Most of all, I am trying to convince readers to get informed before they take out insurance and not to underestimate the risk of not being insured.

MONEY
DO YOU REALLY NEED IT?

W hen you teach finance, there is nothing more disconcerting than hearing someone say, "I don't care about
money." It's as if they are in denial and negligent, not to mention
doomed to financial dependence. People who say money isn't
important to them generally have no assets, spend everything
they have and are counting on luck to get by.

The same people tend to love the book *The Secret*, which
encourages readers to manifest their dreams through vision boards
and wishful thinking. They have benefited so much from the gen-
erosity of the people close to them (their parents, their spouse and
others) that they have never had to worry about their future.

No one truly cares about money, but plenty of people complain they don't have enough. We don't care about money, but
we want to earn more. We don't care about money provided we
can enjoy the pleasures it buys. **No, money doesn't make you
happy. Far from it. But neither does poverty.**

What does it mean to care about money? Apart
from Ebenezer Scrooge, few well-balanced people
get excited just looking at it, touching it or counting

it, particularly in the digital age. In the collective imagination, "caring about money" is often used pejoratively.

But plenty of people enjoy accumulating wealth, planning for their needs and managing expenses, for a variety of reasons. You may be afraid of financial precariousness or uncertainty. You may want your children to have a better life than you had. Luxury can be attractive, even though it can seem rather superficial.

At its essence, what is money? An image may have just popped into your head: coins or, preferably, notes (let's be a little ambitious, even in our imagination). But no, that's not money. Money is trading power. More specifically, it is recognition of a debt.

If you have $1,000 in your wallet, you have an acknowledgement of debt payable to the bearer. For example, if you give a merchant $1,000, the merchant recognizes that he or she has a debt toward you, payable in goods or services. Accepting money means acknowledging a debt to someone else, the exception being charitable donations.

Before money (or its equivalent) existed, people had to barter. The problem with barter lies in structuring it. How do you fairly equate two people's different needs? This is hard to do in an organized, populous society where physical space is limited.

A system based solely on sharing would be the polar opposite of our own. Workers would be taken advantage of by people who aren't as hard-working. How do you make sure everyone does their fair share in the community, if there are no consequences for those who avoid doing it?

Another approach is self-sufficiency. But that raises another problem: in a society as densely populated as ours, not everyone can have their own patch of land to cultivate. The quest for efficiency and the diversification of activities is what helped establish modern society. This organization lets individuals concentrate on a particular area and generate economies of scale, that is, economies of costs based on volume.

Money also lets you postpone fulfilling a need. You can consume when you want, because money doesn't go bad. Rather than working the field and having to harvest vegetables regularly, you can work in an office tower on Monday and spend what you earn three weeks later; thus, you are displacing the exchange of money over time.

Money: a fact of life

Money gives you flexibility in society. Capitalism is an imperfect system, but it sets the rules of the game we play. You can agree or disagree with the rules, you can rebel against them, but you are nonetheless part of the system. To live in a capitalist society, you need to learn the rules of money. **That's what money is: a tool in the game of life.**

Of course, money is not evenly distributed at birth. Blood relations determine your initial wealth, just as they do for a king and his family. People pass wealth down to the next generation, no matter how limited. Inheritance is probably the economic concept that creates the greatest distortion between a person's financial situation and their "worth." Nature gives us certain assets, and inheritance creates another source of discrimination.

Given all of this, can you really say, "I don't care about money"? No. We all need money to pay the rent, buy clothes, eat, travel and whatever else. Money is a tool for transferring value that allows people to concentrate on what they want to do and subcontract what they don't want to do. For instance, I can choose to work more to pay someone to clean my house rather than doing it myself.

Being able to deal with bad luck

Unless you have a crystal ball, you can't live as though tomorrow were your last day on earth. And you can't live as though you are going to live to be 115. But between the two extremes, there is the risk of misfortune, loss of autonomy, psychological distress and chronic illness.

Bad luck strikes at random. We have a hard time accepting that fact. That's why you hear people say things like, "I'd rather enjoy life while I still can and spend it all now."

While this argument may hold true in one sense, it makes absolutely no sense in another. As long as you are able to work, you are able to earn money. But when a major problem strikes and you are no longer independent, you need resources. Being willing to spend thirty years in poverty because you were lazy as a young adult is a mystery to me.

So, money, do you really need it? In North American society, the answer is yes. And the amount you need depends on two simple factors:

1. the income column, which involves effort, and an increase in income, which is not always within your control; and
2. the expense column, which fluctuates depending on your lifestyle.

Take care of your finances

This is the ultimate goal of this book. I'm not trying to get into all the technical aspects of personal finance. I'm trying to show that financial transactions are a fact of life but that we can question consumer dogma. I'm in no way advocating you live like a monk. But there are key budget items to consider and important financial habits you need to adopt when you become an adult.

In Canada, you can become a politician, a doctor, a lawyer or a dentist with no financial knowledge. Money and the systems that govern it are major gaps in our education. Responsible spending and financial management are in the sub-basement of the hierarchy of knowledge.

Trusting service providers and salespeople to determine your needs is like trusting the Big Bad Wolf to design your straw house or asking Lise Watier whether you need a little blush. Companies use different strategies to influence what we consider "basic needs." We aren't as tough and pragmatic as we like to think in the face of all these influences.

The real question you need to ask isn't "Do I really need money?" or "How much money do I need?" The real question is, **"What portion of my money am I spending for no reason? How much of my life have I wasted working to pay for useless stuff?"**

If you think about your possessions in terms of hours worked or vacation days not taken, you will see things from a new, tangible perspective. What am I missing out on to buy myself that thing? No, I'm not going to work the equivalent of two weeks just to be able to wear that coat. And two days of work just to go out for dinner? Hmm, I think I'll repair what I own rather than work overtime to buy new.

If caring about money means:

- ✔ understanding the rules of the game,
- ✔ not being a slave to a job you hate,
- ✔ and having a bit of freedom of choice . . .

then consider me "into money."

Hey, I'm taking some unpaid vacation to go on a little road trip. Want to come along? What do you mean, you can't—are you broke? Oh, sure, bills to pay . . .

Not caring about money isn't so easy, is it?

I know, it sounds crass to talk about money . . . but you really need to!

DEBT
DO YOU REALLY NEED IT?

I have a confession to make: I'm in debt. I can just hear you saying: "What? For real? You of all people!"

Why? Aren't you? There is nothing wrong with debt. Access to credit can be useful: it allows you to invest and shift liquidity across time. Debt lets you engage in economic activity and buy things, such as a house, land or company shares.

The definition of "financially responsible" isn't paying cash for a house or a business. On the other hand, if you go into debt to pay for a new car, new clothes or the latest iPad, you've got off track. Debt can be useful, particularly for building wealth. That's the right track. **So the problem isn't with the word *debt*, but rather how that debt is used.**

Debt for investing

We know that we should use debt only for investing. So what is an investment? It's something that delivers a return.

When your friend tells you he invested in leather seats for his custom Honda Civic, it's not an investment. Unless his custom

Honda Civic becomes a museum piece for the future anthropo-
logical study of the human species (from the Douchebag Era),
it will never increase in value.

Is a house an investment? That is up for debate. But one thing
is certain: the capital gains on a primary residence
don't give rise to taxes, because there is an exemption.
And a home is one of the few ways to force natural-
born spenders to save.

Leverage

Going into debt for leverage is a good idea if—and only if—the
return on the investment is higher than the cost of the debt. The
interest paid on a debt is generally tax deductible if the debt is
used to generate income (except if the investment is tax sheltered
in an RRSP, a TFSA or another tax tool).

For example, if you buy a fiveplex that generates an annual
return of 4 percent, and you pay 3 percent in interest to the bank,
you have created a positive leverage effect. **You are making
money with other people's money.** Leverage is a basic financial
principle.

If it's so simple, why doesn't everyone use leverage? Why
doesn't everyone go into debt to generate a return? Because
investing involves educated guesses.

Shares bought at too high a price can end in a fiasco (does
Nortel ring a bell?). Before taking the plunge, your analysis
needs to suggest the return will be higher than the cost of
borrowing.

If you buy shares, the return may come in the form of a major
capital gain in five, six or ten years. In the meantime, you need
to repay the debt (capital and interest). You aren't earning income

while you are repaying the debt, which means that not everyone can afford to use this strategy.

When it comes to real estate investing, it can all look great on paper, but can change when investors come up against a harsh reality: rising interest rates, tenants who don't pay on time, or a major structural problem and hidden-defect lawsuit that could end up costing more in legal fees than the amount that can be recovered. It's easy not to take into account the old roof that needs replacing, aging brick joints or leaky pipes. And the list goes on.

Basically, real estate investors tend to pay too much for buildings, because they don't properly estimate the renovations that are needed. So the act of investing in real estate isn't the problem, but rather the price paid for a building.

Going into debt to invest doesn't give you a licence to print money. You need to evaluate the price paid, the cost of the debt and your ability to sustain the cash outlays.

Buying on credit?

Without being too rigid, you can stick to a personal rule about debt.

For example, your car is on its last legs, but you haven't had the time or the opportunity to pull together the money you need to buy a used one. Do you go into debt for a few months while you generate the extra cash to pay for it? Why not?

That's the personal rule I set for myself: if I can't pay for a used car within twelve months of buying it, it may be that I don't have the money to buy it. So I choose other options: a cheaper model or another way of getting around.

You can allow yourself a certain amount of leeway when it comes to consumer credit. The danger is when it becomes an automatic way of spending: that's when you become a slave to your payments. The twelve-month rule offers a bit of flexibility.

Here is another example: A big cheque is due to arrive in September, but a "need" arises in June, along with a spending opportunity. If you can match your anticipated income with the expense, you are following the twelve-month use of credit guideline. It's not a universal law, but rather a personal rule of thumb. Basically, sometimes I accept that I need to pay for something before the cash has come in, but no more than one year ahead of time.

When I see ads for sofas you can pay off at just $19.95 per month over twenty-four months, I think that, before doing that, I would buy one second-hand. **It's not rocket science: responsible spending means only buying new when you have saved the money you need.** Why become a slave to payments? If you can't save before spending, doesn't that show that you are living beyond your means?

I know it sounds like I'm lecturing. But if you keep putting on weight, eventually you figure out you need to do something to lose it. So why let debt keep growing until you are backed against the wall—in other words, the morbid obesity of debt—before reacting? In personal finance, declaring bankruptcy is like getting your stomach stapled.

The goal: positive net worth

The logic behind debt is simple. First you need to ask yourself whether more debt will ultimately increase or reduce your net assets. The goal is to keep growing the bottom line: assets minus liabilities. As long as you have positive net assets, you can get by.

Let's take a concrete example. You own a home worth $300,000 and have a mortgage of $200,000. Your net worth is therefore $100,000. This means that, should misfortune strike and you can't make your mortgage payments, and you sell your house, you will have tens of thousands of dollars in your pocket to start over.

The problem is refinancing. Many people dip into the capital on their homes to pay off debt. That's okay when you have to consolidate your debt, because a house offers the cheapest long-term cost of financing.

But repeated refinancing can't be sustained in the long term; the property won't necessarily have increased in value when you need additional financing. In the best of circumstances, when you borrow using a mortgage, it should be to improve or maintain the value of a house, for instance by fixing the balcony or doing major renovations.

The reality of debt

Here is a free tip: **you need to go into debt ONLY to invest.** If you answer no to the question "Would I be able to pay cash for this?" you need to go second-hand to buy what you can afford without financing.

When I hear people say, "Yes, but financing is practically free at 0.9 percent a month," I reply, "That just means that the cost of financing is built into the purchase price." In fact, a rate of 0.9 percent a month is just a way of stroking the customer. It's like telling someone who is obese, "That little black number gives you an hourglass figure." A business can't be financed at that rate. And why would it voluntarily forgo a return? Businesses aren't charities!

Debt and relationships

This is a topic that can lead to heated discussions
at home. Having discipline is great, but your better
half may resist the idea of responsible finances.

One day a woman wrote to me about her exasperation at her
spouse's spending. What do you do when one of the partners
saves for two while the other digs a deep hole of debt? If every
serious discussion leads to flat-out refusals, do you jump ship or
end your days a captain drowned in the pilot house?

You might argue that you would put love before financial con-
siderations. That's fine, but will what is considered an acceptable-
for-now amount of debt eventually end up destroying that love?
Taking care of a relationship starts with sound management of
joint finances. That may seem calculated, but sound management of household debt has its benefits.

MANAGING YOUR INVESTMENTS
DO YOU REALLY NEED TO?

W hen I was young, my neighbour would spend his week-ends obsessively washing his boat and his car. My other neighbour used a toothbrush to get out all the streaks of dirt left on his shiny brown car. (Yes, brown cars used to be in style.)

Today, people brag about spending three hours on the phone with their mobile service provider to get them to drop the price of their plan by $8.13 a month.

For the past thirty years, we have been investing a lot of time in managing our day-to-day lives and our stuff. But when it comes to managing our investments, we have no interest in understanding products and analyzing, maintaining and opti-mizing them. We are prepared to spend half a day at a car dealer-ship in the suburbs to buy 2,000 kilos of metal, but when it comes to planning for the future, it's another story.

Discouraged experts
Talking to financial planners, investment advisers and mutual fund advisers is sobering. They tell me about the reality of their jobs and how discouraged

they are by the lack of personal responsibility among "investors."

Some clients want to save, but when they are asked how much they want to set aside every month, they often aren't prepared to do the budget exercise to figure it out. It's like being at a car dealership and saying, "I want to buy a car, but I don't know what model or how much I want to spend. Actually, I don't even know whether I need a car, but I'm here, so serve me, and make it snappy."

It's February 26. There are only a few days left to make an RRSP contribution for last year. Some clients are in a rush and want it all wrapped up in fifteen minutes over their lunch hour.

These latecomers write a cheque for $5,000 to a mutual fund adviser, quickly sign the papers and get back to their lives. These are the same clients who, when they buy a paintbrush at the hardware store, take the time to ask the clerk whether it's good for latex paint and inquire about other tools that will make their lives easier. We complain that we are being sold financial products we don't understand, but at the same time we treat financial industry professionals with less regard than we would a paintbrush salesperson.

Do you ever look into what kind of investments you have? Or the returns you've earned to date? Or your expectations for growth? Having an inappropriate investment strategy can make a difference between actual and potential returns.

Of course, it's great to manage your investments, but you need capital in the first place to implement a strategy to earn a return. When a client starts saving for retirement at age forty-five or fifty, advisers are as discouraged as a heart surgeon who sees her overweight patient eat a large foie gras poutine while smoking a cigarette, just two weeks after a quadruple bypass. It's never too late to start saving, but the longer you wait, the more disappointing the results. It's simple math.

Not caring about returns has a cost

I couldn't write a book on personal finance without explaining the principle of compound interest. I know, you've seen examples of it time and time again. But if you bought this book, the information may have gone in one ear and out the other.

Here is a simple example.

Jean-Philippe and Karine are 25-year-olds who studied in the same field. Neither has an employer pension plan. They each save $5,000 a year.

Without taking into account inflation or other sources of retirement income, how much will each of them have accumulated at age sixty-five, assuming that Jean-Philippe wants a return of 4 percent and Karine is aiming for 6 percent?

At age sixty-five, Jean-Philippe will have around $475,000.

At age sixty-five, Karine will have around $774,000.

How is such a wide gap possible? Because Karine was more aggressive in managing her personal finances.

The average annual rate of return, the level of risk and the investment period explain the difference between the two investors. In this example, Jean-Philippe and Karine's contributions to their RRSP are constant, but they could also gradually increase them as their salaries rise.

The risk of the risk-free investment

You need to get used to risk. You need to understand that saving from an early age using GICs—or, as I call them, guaranteed indigence certificates—doesn't let investors make above-average returns. Worse still, in the long term, this sort of strategy generally doesn't even keep up with inflation. Investing like a nervous Nellie means ending up poorer. **Without a doubt, neglecting your investment strategy means choosing to end up poorer.**

Financial institutions can put all the sexy names they want on risk-free and reduced-risk investments, but that doesn't change the fact that there is a ceiling on their return. Why? Because people want guaranteed protection of their capital, and guarantees have a cost. An investment that guarantees capital isn't free: the cost of that guarantee is included in the return on investment.

Over a forty-year investment horizon, it is hard to believe that an investment in an index fund or shares in quality companies won't deliver returns that are higher than guaranteed capital, even given the greater volatility.

 For example, if you had invested $1,000 in 1980, is guaranteeing your capital all that important if you plan to withdraw it in 2020? It is highly unlikely that shares held for forty years yield a return lower than $1,000, unless you socked all your money into Nortel.

Managing your investments also means not worrying about day-to-day volatility in their value. If, after a few years, you have $200,000 invested, don't panic if one day it drops by $2,000. That's only a 1 percent drop in the value of your portfolio.

Paradigm shift

When I signed my contract, my editor told me he didn't want to see the word *paradigm* in the book. I'm using it as a header to see whether he's paying attention.

It's not the temporary loss of capital that investors want to avoid, but not generating a return. When investors who take no risk brag that they didn't lose any money in a stock market correction, they are often forgetting a basic principle. Investors who exposed themselves to a greater risk may have lost 10 percent of their assets in the short term, but cumulatively, they have probably lost, temporarily, the return that other investors didn't earn.

Let's take the case of Geneviève and Pierre, both age thirty-five. Geneviève has never lost any capital, because she has always invested in risk-free products. Pierre buys stocks and mutual funds.

They each had $50,000 in investments a few years ago. Before the last stock market correction, Geneviève's investments were worth $60,000 and Pierre's were worth $78,000.

Today, Pierre is a bit discouraged: the TSX lost 10 percent of its value recently. So he lost 10 percent of his portfolio, leaving him with a balance of $70,200.

Geneviève, on the other hand, is happy: her investments are worth more than the capital she invested. She tells her friends how proud she is: "I was prudent, and it paid off; I didn't lose any money in the stock market correction."

Pierre cracks a smile. "I temporarily lost $7,800, but that's from past returns you didn't earn. So I still have more net assets than you."

What this example shows is that by being afraid to lose capital, you forget the fear of failing to earn a return. We should be trying to make what we save grow. Basically, total savings generally depend on three variables:

1. the capital invested;
2. the annual return; and
3. the investment period.

Focusing on protecting capital is not a good strategy in the long term.

Obviously, the older you are, the more you need to reduce your exposure to risk. But in the initial years of saving, you need a different investment strategy than someone who is seventy-one and about to move their RRSP into a registered retirement income fund (RRIF).

If you are twenty-five and have the same investment strategy as someone with a fluffy toilet seat cover, it may be a sign that you're on the wrong track.

Neglecting your investments contributes to financial precariousness. When you have $500,000 saved, one year with a 10 percent return is the equivalent for some people of a year of working forty hours a week. If you ignore the return on your investments, without realizing it you are making them grow less than they would if you were comfortable with risk.

So, managing your investments: do you really need to? It depends on whether or not you like working and saving for nothing.

NB: This chapter is intended to illustrate the correlation between risk and return, but should not be considered personalized advice. **Always consult a professional before investing based on your investor profile.**

CHILDREN'S PARTIES
DO YOU REALLY NEED THEM?

Martin and Isabelle are stressed out. Are they getting married? No. Today is their son Victor's birthday, and they are expecting his twenty-four kinda-sorta friends.

The couple has it all planned: a bouncy castle has been rented, a magician will arrive around 1 p.m., loot bags have been purchased for every guest, a referee/coach has been hired for the afternoon soccer game. They're ready!

The sushi will be delivered at 11:45, and the pool temperature is at 26 degrees Celsius. The gluten-free cake was made by the vegetarian baker using organic flour. **Victor's party has to be perfect, because his friend Gabriel had acrobats, and the kids loved that.**

This fictional case shows a bit of the insanity that bouncy castles bring to children's birthday parties. It's even worse if your child is friends with the child of a rich entrepreneur. The children's party planners will be rubbing their hands with delight.

One day a friend of mine who lives in an affluent suburb of Montreal had a party for his daughter and her friends. As the party was ending, the mother of a guest asked my friend, "My daughter really enjoyed herself. What was the activity?"

"We played hide-and-seek," he replied.

My friend had taken care of the children himself: no bouncy castle, no magician, no emcee. He just entertained his daughter and her friends, something that is fairly uncommon, it seems.

What greater joy is there for children than when you play with them and take an interest in them? I don't remember ever having as much fun as when my father played with me or came to watch me play soccer.

Children's birthday parties, adult parties, receptions and other occasions create a (false) sense of pride that we are giving our guests more, when we are actually overdoing it. The comparisons start: when the neighbours serve you foie gras, you can't have them over for hot dogs.

Our friend brought over a $30 bottle of wine the last time, so we can't offer her a drink from an $18 bottle. It all serves to create a bubble of increased spending, quantities and needs, and we get stuck in a cycle of imperfect relativism.

Children's parties organized by party planners: do you really need them? No. You just need a little time. Because time is precious. You can't accumulate it or generate a return on it in minutes. It is limited, finite. Isn't your time the greatest gift you can give? Besides, if you are willing to spend hundreds of dollars on your child's birthday but you don't contribute to his or her RESP, you are missing the boat.

THE NO-GIFT PACT
DO YOU REALLY NEED IT?

I n our society, any pretext can be used for giving a gift. We give them for all sorts of reasons and on all sorts of occasions: wedding gifts, hostess gifts, thank-you gifts, retirement gifts, work anniversary gifts, birthday gifts, end-of-school-year gifts, Valentine's Day gifts . . . and the list goes on. No one dares stop this incessant game of shuffling resources back and forth; social conventions are hard to change.

Christmas: a zero-sum game

I hate Christmas. Call me the Grinch, but I hate the festival of needless spending. **The magic number is $652.[1] That was the average holiday budget for Canadian households in 2015.** The word *budget* obviously means forecast spending; there is nothing to say that it will be respected or that the amount is actually available.

This chapter is taken in part from one of my blog posts on Voir.ca.

1   www.journaldemontreal.com/2015/12/01/le-quebec-depense-moins-que-toutes-lesautres-provinces-pour-noel

Christmas is a period of orgiastic consumption during which modern society demonstrates its decadence at its most ridiculous, laughable and appalling. One wonders whether North Americans aren't just bored. We spend to relieve boredom. Buying for the sake of buying becomes a habit. "Bought any new toys lately? Are you thinking of buying anything?"

Then there are all the gift exchanges where people buy yet another thing they don't really need. One more thing to shove in a box, a closet or a garage, all of them already filled to bursting. Eventually, this useless stuff ends up in a garage sale. And with it the sequined dress worn only once and the bright-red shirt exclusively for the holidays.

What if . . .

. . . we took a break? A giftless Christmas. A Christmas where we can wear comfortable old jeans, drink the tail ends of forty-ounce bottles of booze, and beam with pleasure while we watch time go by.

What is most precious, and what we no longer give ourselves, is not the latest tech toy or cellphone. What has become scarce in our crazy lives is time. Giving our time.

I've always found the Christmas holidays wonderful when we take the time to just be, to share, and to enjoy time with the people we care about. Nothing extravagant, no trips south or ski weekends at Jay Peak. Just the time to say to family and friends, "I love you, you are important to me, and I'm glad to be with you."

Taking the time to stop, to put the brakes on a hectic life.

Taking the time to make a coffee at home rather than contributing to a multinational's tax evasion.

Rediscovering the pleasure of childhood.

Taking part in simple activities that don't cost anything: going skating in the park, going for a walk in the evening, lying in the snow and looking at the stars (a pipe dream if you live in Montreal, where light pollution obscures the sky).

Basically, taking a bite out of life at its most basic. Taking the time to live before we die.

What if every year we signed the *no-gift pact*? A mutual agreement to spend more quality time as a family rather than giving each other material things. **Let's make a resolution to stem the madness, one family at a time.** Let's avoid sales, lineups, cars packed with stuff, Boxing Day, the stress of travelling in snowstorms, the time spent wrapping gifts. Let's say no to the madness and just take time for ourselves.

The irony of the holidays

A few years ago, I was working for an international accounting firm in downtown Montreal. It was December 23. I was overwhelmed by my professional life and my lack of a personal life. I was going as fast as time would allow and flirting with permanent fatigue. As I was on my way home one evening, a man approached me not far from the Berri–UQAM metro station.

"Spare some change for something to eat?"

"No, sorry."

I kept going. Then a few steps farther, I stopped and went back.

"What do you want to eat?"

"Whatever you want to give me."

It turned out he wanted McDonald's. I went into the restaurant with him. The employees watched as I walked in with the guy. They were used to seeing him outside, wearing plastic bags instead of boots. I bought him a Big Mac combo and a gift card (this one made sense) for his next meal. He thanked me and I left.

One wonders who did whom a favour that day. I felt as if I was of more use to that person in that moment than to all the clients at the firm I had been working for since my career started.

Since that time, once a year, I make it a point to help someone, anonymously, without sharing it on social media, with no video of a bucket of ice water over my head. I help because I want to recognize the man in the mirror every morning. The mirror doesn't always reflect what we want. Helping your fellow human being is in the end kind of a selfish act, because it lets you love yourself.

For Christmas, I'm dreaming of empty shopping centres, children happy to see their parents play with them rather than buy themselves a bit of peace and quiet. I dream of something different. What about you? Why not give your Christmas to a food bank? Use that $652 to buy non-perishable goods, or give it to another cause that is close to your heart.

Gift cards

They abound in stores. From a purely economic point of view, they are a strange concept. What are we actually doing when we buy a gift card? We are exchanging Canadian dollars, a universally accepted currency, for $50 that can be spent only at, say, Sport Chek.

Why not just give the person $50? Because it's just not done? To make sure the person doesn't use it to buy something else? Giving a gift card is false good conscience: it only seems like a personal gift.

We buy these cards for a reason: they buy you peace. The giver doesn't spend hours looking for a gift, and the recipient is happy to be able to choose a gift rather than have to return something. Financially speaking, it's getting ridiculous: I give you a $50 gift card to spend at Canadian Tire and you give me a $50 gift card for Rona.

Basically, we end up in a zero-sum game, wasting our time.

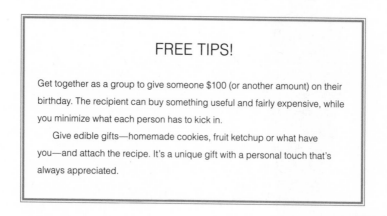

FREE TIPS!

Get together as a group to give someone $100 (or another amount) on their birthday. The recipient can buy something useful and fairly expensive, while you minimize what each person has to kick in.

Give edible gifts—homemade cookies, fruit ketchup or what have you—and attach the recipe. It's a unique gift with a personal touch that's always appreciated.

Space in a home is at a premium. Filling it with objects makes free space even more valuable. Why not agree among rational adults to limit the number of gifts?

So, who wants to sign the *no-gift pact*? Who knows, you may even learn to like it. Because one more doodad: do you really need it?

A SPENDING STRATEGY
DO YOU REALLY NEED IT?

A spending strategy? "What are you talking about?" you may ask. Obviously, we all have our ways of choosing one product over another. We all know a wise older person who shows us how work should be done: how to fix a house, plant a garden or jerry-rig something. When we're thinking about buying something, we all have a know-it-all friend or uncle who can tell us everything there is to know about any product under the sun.

But we don't have anyone to tell us how to control our spending. This chapter is not especially scientific, but it offers a three-point strategy for buying expensive products.

1. Go home
Consumption is like lust. It stops us from thinking straight, and drains the blood from our brains. We want the thing in front of us, right now. There is nothing rational about it; it's a sudden desire. When I want to make a major purchase and I haven't thought it through, I make myself go home before buying anything. Most of the time,

taking a first look at something tempting and then going back home allows reason to take hold again.

I used to want to buy more guitars than I needed. I don't know why, but when I go into a music store, I have an overwhelming urge to buy a guitar. Is it because I'm a wannabe rock star? It's an impulse, a form of excitement. I see the guitar, I touch it, and as if I've caught a virus, I have a burning desire to buy it.

Yet I already have enough guitars at home for my meagre talent. So going home works well. Once I get home, the desire for another guitar passes, particularly when I see the other three collecting dust.

It's the same principle with bikes. I've had the same bike for twenty years. But every year, I go into a bike shop and tell myself this is the year I'll buy a new one. I talk to the salesperson. I talk the price down. In the end, I go back home and ask myself, "Do you really need it?" The answer is no, mine still works just fine.

Going home before buying something also gives you a chance to make a list of your priority expenses. Most of the time, the impulse to spend is soon a mere memory. Why am I driven to spend? What is missing in my life that this need comes back again and again?

Like a fly drawn to honey, we suck up products ad infinitum, or until we die. We are flies, and products are sugar (or sometimes shit). We just need to be aware of our dependence and talk ourselves down by going home and drinking a green tea.

2. The budget

This may seem obvious, but a strategy that works well is to set yourself a budget before making any purchases. In stores, you can get swept up in the excitement of the moment, and desire grows

exponentially. You feel as though you deserve the best. By deciding in advance on the top price you are willing to pay,
you prevent your brain from short-circuiting when you
are looking at the object of your desire.

For example, you go to the electronics store to buy a TV, and
you set out with a budget of $1,000. Be on your guard—there
will always be a more expensive product with more features. We
tend to notice after the fact that the only feature we really need
is the screen.

To distract you from your real needs, retailers showcase attractive, more expensive models, playing with contrasts and colours.
But since you had the presence of mind to set a budget before
leaving home, you won't fall into their trap.

I would like to meet someone who has actually used all the
features on their television or all thirteen cycles on their washing
machine. There is a serious gap between the possibilities products offer and the time we can devote to them.

3. The pet expenditure category

We all tend to have our favourite spending category. For a long
time, mine was music. I allowed myself a higher budget than
most people to buy compact discs and musical instruments.

Indulging in our belief that happiness is tied to spending, we
allow ourselves to spend more in an area where others wouldn't
spend anything, provided we limit our spending in other budget
areas. Obviously, it's all a question of means. Some people will tell
you that it depends on the amount allocated to that "excessive"
expenditure category, because, if the amount is reasonable, we
could pick two, three or four categories where we let ourselves go
a little wild. It's all a matter of the budget and financial control.

One thing is certain: believing that we *deserve* the most expensive, highest-end product is strange. Why should others settle for less, when we are treating ourselves to a luxury product? The words *deserve it* have always sounded odd to me. As if spending has anything to do with deserving. "I work hard. I'll treat myself!" If you catch yourself thinking that way, you need to take a good hard look at things. Why work so much if the ultimate goal is to reward yourself for having worked too much?

The strategy can be summed up as H-B-C: home, budget and category.

1. Take your time before buying.
2. Determine the actual utility of the thing.
3. Make sure you're not spoiling yourself in every expenditure category

There is no perfect strategy when it comes to spending, but as Benjamin Franklin said, "by failing to prepare, you are preparing to fail."

So, a spending strategy: do you really need it? Not necessarily, but it can be helpful. Going home first, having a budget in mind and deciding on a discretionary spending category helps you keep a cool head when the impulse to buy strikes.

MANAGING EXPECTATIONS
DO YOU REALLY NEED TO?

A h, managing expectations. We are endlessly managing expectations, whether in our relationship, our career, the projects we take on or our leisure activities. Managing expectations is universal, including in personal finance and lifestyle. Not managing expectations in these two areas is a recipe for unhappiness.

The expectation equation

Forgive the accounting metaphor, but managing expectations is a lot like analyzing financial results. Sound ridiculous? Bear with me.

When analyzing financial results, we calculate the variance between the actual result and the forecast result. For example, we would use the following equation to calculate the spread, in percentage terms, between results and the forecast:

Gap between results and expectations (as a percentage)

$$\frac{(\text{Real financial results} - \text{Forecast financial results}) \times 100}{\text{Forecast financial results}}$$

$$= \frac{(\$1{,}000 - \$900) \times 100}{900}$$

$$= 11.11\%$$

248

If the solution to the equation is positive, this means we have exceeded sales or profit forecasts. Management and shareholders are satisfied, since we exceeded expectations. (When we're talking about expenditure categories, the logic is generally reversed, unless additional spending generated proportionately higher revenue.)

Corporate executives have become masters at managing expectations to satisfy markets and investors.

In our personal lives, it's sort of the same principle. Let's take an example: A woman goes home. She prepares for a romantic evening. She takes a shower, chills some wine, makes a simple dinner and lights candles.

Her expectations are mounting. The phone rings and her boyfriend says he's going to spend the evening working on a file for the next day (in soap operas, it's always a file we never learn anything about, because it's usually empty). So the equation is:

Gap between results and expectations (as a percentage)
$$\frac{(\text{Value of an evening of television} - \text{Value of a romantic evening}) \times 100}{\text{Value of a romantic evening}}$$
= Negative result because an evening of television generally has less value than a romantic evening

Measure the satisfaction. If the result is 0, it means that our needs have been satisfied. If it is more than 0 percent, it means we have exceeded expectations. If it is negative, we didn't achieve expectations.

It's hard to put a number to the result, but you can appreciate that the value of the evening spent in front of the television is lower than the value of a romantic evening. Satisfaction is therefore negative. Some situations are easier to quantify—for example, salary expectations or the value of a home.

You may think my perspective is too steeped in accounting or mathematics, but as I explained, it's a metaphor. If expectations are just barely satisfied, the variance between the actual outcome and expectations will be 0 percent.

So, in practical terms, we can define happiness as the extent to which an expectation was satisfied. We can't really put a figure on that satisfaction, but we can assign an order of magnitude (equal to, greater than or less than, better or worse than expectations). We don't always control the numerator in the equation (the actual result), but we can concentrate on the denominator, that is, our expectations.

Concrete examples

- ✔ If I ask my employer for a 30 percent raise, it's highly likely I'll be disappointed if I only get 2 percent.
- ✔ The same principle applies to expectations in relationships. If I tell my spouse that I will be home at 6 p.m., she will be disappointed if I arrive at 8 p.m. But if I tell her I will be home at 8:30 p.m. and I manage to get there at 8:15 p.m., she will be pleased. It's all in managing expectations, which avoids major disappointments. The goal is to control the denominator in the equation.
- ✔ If one of my expectations were to live in a $1 million single-family home in Outremont but all I could afford was a $250,000 condo in Hochelaga-Maisonneuve, I might be disappointed.

Why all the disappointment? Because of poorly managed expectations. The anticipated results were too hard to achieve. These examples show that objectives need to be properly defined.

Expectations and SMART objectives

In management, there is a way of formulating objectives that also applies to our personal lives, particularly in terms of managing expectations. To achieve your goals, you need to know what they are.

In my early twenties, I wrote my life's goals on a piece of paper I carried in my wallet for a few years. As a commitment to myself, I had decided to set goals based on my expectations, interests, desires, dreams and abilities. The list was divided into several categories, including:

- ✔ Investments
- ✔ Savings
- ✔ Physical fitness
- ✔ Family
- ✔ Career

If you don't set goals, you don't get anywhere, or at least not where you want to be. For example, in the savings section, my goal was to save 20 percent of my gross salary every year. In the career section I wrote down different objectives, such as "become a full university professor by age forty-five" and "write a book by age forty."

The goals all made sense; they followed the principles from my management courses. They were what are called SMART objectives. What are SMART objectives?

Specific. A well-defined objective must be clear and precise. For example, "become a better person" is vague. But "become a full university professor" is clear and precise.

Measurable. You need to be able to quantify the objective to determine whether it has been attained. For example, if my objective is to "save 18 percent of my annual salary," that's measurable. You can measure whether or not the goal was achieved at the end of the year.

Ambitious. When it comes to managing expectations, the initial objective still has to be ambitious, which is to say hard enough to achieve to be satisfying. Ambition depends on one's own capabilities. For example, "get my high school diploma before age thirty" isn't ambitious for the head of the class, but it may be for someone going back to school as an adult.

Realistic. Obviously, an objective needs to be achievable. A lack of realism is not only discouraging, it can also hamper our management of expectations. For example, "become president of a multinational by age twenty-five" is possible, but when you're twenty-four and flipping burgers at McDonald's, it doesn't make that much sense. Or if you earn $40,000 a year as an employee, it may be unrealistic to want to retire at age forty.

Time-bound. The objective must be defined in time. To achieve an objective and track it, you need to have a timetable. For example, wanting to "buy a revenue property by age thirty" is a timely objective, because there is a clear deadline. If, at age thirty-two, you are still a tenant, you are behind on the time-bound portion of your objective.

So, when you set personal or professional goals, they need to adhere to these five principles to allow you to manage your expectations. The following goal is an example of a properly worded one:

> Save 20 percent (**measurable, ambitious and realistic**) of my annual gross salary (**specific**) from age 25 to 65 (**time-bound**).

By setting SMART objectives, you ensure that expectations are both realistic and ambitious. Managing expectations doesn't mean setting such modest objectives that you take no pride in achieving them. Managing expectations means striking a balance between realism and ambition.

Most Canadians don't contribute the maximum allowable to an RRSP. So it's relatively ambitious for the average person to contribute 18 percent of the previous year's income (less the pension adjustment), but it is realistic to make a few choices that are different from those of other taxpayers. Expectations and objectives are closely linked, which is something you should be aware of.

Changing objectives and expectations

Another important principle for managing expectations is recognizing that objectives and expectations are constantly changing. They need to be adjusted as life takes different turns, for better or for worse.

It may be that what was realistic at age twenty is no longer so at thirty-five or forty-five. As time goes by, interests and objectives can change. For example, I wanted to be a university professor, and I became a CEGEP (college) teacher. I ended up achieving my professional goal, just at a different level.

Over time, I saw that this twist in my career path was beneficial overall. Changing my expectations contributed to my personal happiness.

Reviewing and taking action

Personal and professional lives have a major thing in common: if you don't make decisions, others will make them for you and tell you where to go.

I like to use the metaphor of a sailboat on the ocean. If the captain has no destination, the boat will be carried along by the waves and go around in circles, navigating in the most favourable direction. But a captain with a destination will do everything possible to get there, even if the winds aren't favourable.

So, you periodically need to ask yourself, "Where am I with respect to my personal and professional goals?" and "What do I need to do to achieve them?" When I had a bit of time on my hands and was procrastinating, I would ask myself what I had done today, or in the past year, to achieve one of my goals.

Taking stock of your goals from time to time means being aware that time is passing and that you can adjust your course if necessary.

OBJECTIVE: Retire at sixty-five with an annual income equal to 70 percent of your salary.

REVIEWING THE OBJECTIVE:
- ✔ Is the amount saved monthly consistent with the objective?
- ✔ Did you meet with a professional to create a retirement plan?

ACTIONS: You may have always dreamed of changing jobs, but instead you put down roots in your cubicle, performing menial tasks for twenty years without doing anything to break free of the inertia. As my mother used to say, "The Lord helps those who help themselves."

We tend to wait for good things to drop from the sky, to receive the offer that changes our lives without us making any effort. If you let yourself become "cubiclized," the cubiclizers will just keep acting the way they do. So what do you need to do to achieve your goal or to reposition yourself in order to achieve it?

Happiness and healthy management of expectations

The management of expectations is intimately tied to the goals we set in every area of our lives.

Not managing expectations and not taking concrete action to achieve your goals means settling for dissatisfaction.

I tend to define happiness as the midpoint between no regrets and no remorse. You have to be sure you don't regret having done nothing and that you don't have remorse about the choices you did make. Managing expectations limits regrets and prevents remorse.

I know, sound management of expectations is easier said than done. But to avoid ending up as a passenger in the car of your own life, you need a plan.

Managing expectations: do you really need to? Question asked, question answered.

TRAVEL
DO YOU REALLY NEED IT?

I can hear your teeth gnashing as you read the title of this chapter. Your blood pressure is rising, and you want to insult me on Facebook. You've already started drafting the message.

Rest assured that in essence I agree with you: it's nice to travel, to explore new horizons, to experience another world, and to learn, live and question. I mean, can't we have any fun at all? Yes. But it may be time to talk about our obsession with travel.

Travel is like icing: first you have to have baked a cake to spread it on. Savings are the cake. **The mindset of "travel now, save later" is all well and good, but in a few years that neglect will cost you.** Financial neglect is like compound interest: over the years, its impact grows exponentially.

Treating yourself to a trip isn't an achievement; it's an expense, just like a hot tub in the backyard (fine, with the addition of a brief new experience and memories for a lifetime). Travel is merely a financial choice. You allocate part of your budget to the flight and to the food and accommodations in another part of the world.

It's not an accomplishment; it's a luxury that means a smaller RRSP contribution in a given year. **While you're in Italy, are you eating your retirement?** I hope that plate of pasta was good, because it's going to cost a lot more than 15 euros.

Putting travel back into perspective

One day, I was correcting student assignments at a local café. At the table across from me, a woman in her early twenties was giving an interview to a journalist about her travels. She explained that, while travelling, she met all sorts of people who put her up, fed her and so on.

Basically, the message was, "I don't want to work like everyone else. I'm part of something bigger. I'm going to spend my life travelling. Work isn't for me. I'll work just enough to travel."

She looked down on the society we live in, with its wrongheaded values and materialism (or at least that's what it sounded like). Being tied down with children and a home didn't interest her. Perhaps it was a momentary display of the arrogant naïveté of youth, but I could see the journalist feeling judged for her life in a suburban bungalow.

It's fine for the young woman to look down on our structured world, but it's that world that builds the planes that take her places. It's also that world that processes and ships the food she eats and the materials used for her travel gear.

Plus, staying with people like a parasite while travelling is easy enough when you are a young woman in your early twenties. It's a lot harder later on. Travel can shape our youth, but there is a limit to how long you can rely on the economic reality of young people to justify crashing with other people.

Who do you travel for?

I have serious questions for you.

When you go on a trip, who are you really doing it for? Is it just because of peer pressure, so you can say you've gone somewhere?

In your heart of hearts, what is it you want to see? Do you do it because you really want to, or for social acceptance? You may make your friends jealous, but they won't admire you for it.

Why do you take 12,350 pictures on your trip? I hope it's not for your friends. Honestly, we are happy that you had such a good time, but fifteen minutes of looking at your pictures is about all we can take.

What's behind your desire to spend money in tourist traps in other countries?

You're too good for ordinary life? One person's ordinary is another person's extraordinary. That's why you just went to visit another country's ordinary.

DO YOU REALLY NEED IT?

> Who are you running from, tourist attraction to tourist attraction, like a chicken with your head cut off?

> When someone asks you, "Where are you going for your vacation?" aren't you ever tempted to answer, "Nowhere"?

> That sweet feeling of being on vacation, which is to say not at work but enjoying the days without rushing, speed or stress: why can't a staycation be an option?

> Perhaps you travel to realize how good you have it at home. But what are you trying to escape when you take off abroad every time you have five days clear? Your girlfriend or boyfriend you don't really love? Your relationship? Your job? Your thoughts? Gotcha.

Somewhere deep down, we all want to do it. Take off, and leave the daily grind and real life behind. Sometimes we think we are destined for something greater than others. We all think that.

But what is really so special about us?

The need to feel different? The need to feel alive? Maybe. Believe me, I do get it. The thing is, the possibilities of travel are endless, but money is not.

The economic downside of travel
By travelling a lot, globetrotters increase the demand for international flights, making airlines profitable and helping democratize air travel.

In 2014, 3.3 billion people on the planet travelled by plane.[1] But air travel is highly polluting. Putting a machine in the air with that many passengers and their luggage requires enormous power, which has to be maintained throughout the flight.

This creates economic externalities: We are polluting the atmosphere without paying the real price. Our budding globe-trotters, with their appetite for discovery, are contributing to an increase in air traffic and pollution, and ultimately doing harm to society.

Student travel

There is something a little peculiar about humanitarian travel and student travel. Sure, it's great to give young people the opportunity to travel. But from a purely economic point of view, something about it just doesn't make sense. Fundraising activities target family, friends, shoppers at the grocery store and whoever else can be approached. Basically, people who don't have the money to travel themselves are being asked to pay for part of a young person's trip. So, financially speaking, the students seek to have their travel subsidized.

There are also positive aspects of this sort of trip: seeing the world, learning about the gap between rich and poor, and gaining cultural sensitivity. But still, organizing students to raise funds for travel opportunities reinforces the message that others will pay for the things we want.

---

1   www.ledevoir.com, under the "Économie" tab, then the "Actualités économiques" tab, read the article "Le nombre de voyageurs transportés par avion a atteint 3,3 milliards en 2014," online February 7, 2015.

STUDYING TO WORK IN THE TRAVEL INDUSTRY

Your passion for travel may lead you to want to work in the travel industry. But do you really want to sell trips in an agency? What's the difference between selling trips or five-course meals? You're not actually travelling; you're just in sales.

You get a free trip every year? Great! But why not just get a better-paying job and take one trip a year at full price? Sometimes, economic substance must prevail over legal form (that one's for the accountants). In other words, you shouldn't choose your field of study based on travel; you should choose your field of study and travel with it.

It makes me think of university programmes like international commerce. The name contains the word *international*, but what job do you actually get with it? It may sound sexy, but the reality is another story. You really think you'll travel more? That you'll be able to live abroad? What is the demand on the job market for the skill set of being able to pack a carry-on and being impervious to jet lag?

Can you study international accounting? No, accounting exists everywhere, and the standards are international. So, run-of-the-mill accountants can travel for work if they so desire. To work abroad, there is no need for a degree pimped up with the word *international*.

I love to travel

Virtually everyone wants to travel. I want to travel more often. **But at my age, you need to be rich, careless or a tax evader to travel regularly.** Responsible financial life is expensive. It's okay to have a predilection for adventure, but it's just a fact that some people have too many obligations and too much debt to travel.

When it comes to personal finance, as long as you have two years' salary put away by age thirty-five, you're fine. What? Two years' salary? Are you insane? Even with low returns, it is mathematically feasible—unless you're in the habit of drinking away your savings on the beach.

So, you're thirty-five, and you have a great Facebook page with plenty of memories on it. Way to go! And what about your RRSP, TFSA and RESP? How are they doing? Travel, you really need it—but at what cost? I know, I know, I'm boring. But give a little thought to your future . . .

COOKING
DO YOU REALLY NEED TO?

There is a faded sticker on the sweating window of a restaurant that says, "Just Eat." Go ahead, my little piggies, don't even go to the effort of chopping a vegetable or stirring the soup. Just eat. It's so easy. Eat anything you want until your taste buds wear right out.

Thousands of years of making meals ourselves to wind up at a place where humanity is more passive, culinarily speaking. And what is the price of "just eating"? Too high. Not to mention the lack of control over what's on your plate.

Not cooking will put you in the poorhouse. You need to ask yourself what you could have done with the misallocated funds. **Speaking personally, of all the monthly budget items ripe for cutting, eating out is number one.**

But the thing is, people are basically gregarious—we like to go to cafés to see people, enjoy a change of scenery or relax to the ambient music. There's an appeal to being somewhere other than home.

When I lived in a dark, uninviting apartment, I was constantly escaping it. I would tell myself that once I had a nice home, I would spend more time there. It was wishful thinking. The routine of life at home, particularly for someone who works there, can start to feel like a prison.

Restaurants

You need to spend a lot to eat well when you go out. Restaurant owners need to have a big-enough margin to pay for rent, permits, taxes, electricity, salaries, benefits, insurance, raw materials, equipment, maintenance, decor and cleaning. Plus they have to pay themselves enough to cover the hours they put in. When you cook at home, you absorb a large part of those costs.

The real costs associated with cooking at home are the raw materials, the energy and your time (which you could have spent making money).

Without entirely denying yourself the pleasure of eating out, it is a good idea to limit how often you do so. You have to consider the cost of subcontracting cooking and the price of the pleasure of eating a meal away from home.

But be assured that from a strictly financial point of view, restaurants are a poor choice. Diners generate a gross profit for the restaurant owner. They pay more than the price of the meal; they pay for the owner's car and condo.

If we're honest with ourselves, restaurant food isn't always great, it's expensive, and, in the long term, there are health costs—for the individual and for the health care system—associated with the practice. Plus, they provide unfair competition to food you make at home, where we don't cheat as much on sugar, salt, MSG and other questionable products. Their meals may seem tastier, but taste buds often deceive you.

Cafés

At age eighteen, I arrived in Montreal to share an apartment that was clean but located in a boring neighbourhood: Parc-Extension.

Haunting cafés wasn't an option for me, being on a budget. The school year was limited to attending classes, studying and working. There were three of us in a two-bedroom apartment. A folding door split the living room in half to create a third bedroom that could accommodate a single bed.

Using my former situation as a point of comparison, I am always astounded to see university students cry poor as they take over the Starbucks, Second Cups and Van Houttes of the world. I know, it's a simplistic statement. I won't go so far as to say they're living #thegoodlife, but they aren't exactly allocating resources the way they could be.

When you go into a café on a day off, have you ever asked yourself what all those people hanging around actually do? Obviously, you're not the only one with a day off.

To soak up the ambience, I'm writing this in a café. Beside me, a student is trying to study. Unfortunately, she is spending every other minute on social media. In the time she has been here, she has ordered a panini with a salad and two coffees. Since coffees here cost between $2 and $5.45, and her plate costs $10, plus tax and tip, no matter how meagre, the cost of her being here is more than $20.

At home, she could have eaten the same meal for $5 or less. That $15 difference is nothing to sneeze at. Particularly since that $15 is an after-tax expense. Students may have the advantage of a low tax rate, but their financial resources are limited.

Conclusion: the more financially comfortable you are, the greater the cost of subcontracting cooking; food is paid with your net salary. However, the higher your income, the more discretionary budget you have to pay for the luxury of subcontracting.

Drive-throughs

Have you ever watched the lineup of cars waiting to buy coffee at the local fast-food restaurant? Perhaps you're part of the line? Drive-through users claim they are in too much of a rush to make coffee at home.

Honestly, pouring homemade coffee into a travel mug is probably the easiest habit to adopt. I've never understood how drivers can be enraged at the price of gas, but put wear and tear on their brakes at the Tim Hortons drive-through.

When the price of gas increases by 10 cents a litre, it generates public debate. For a 50-litre tank, this increase is less than $1 a day. Eating breakfast or making a cup of coffee at home could offset this increase. The profit for oil refiners is an insult to our collective intelligence, but the profit the coffee merchants make is the result of high-quality service provided (#sarcasm).

Full-service restaurants

Restaurants with service cost 30 percent too much right out of the gate, not even taking into account the owner's gross profit. With taxes totalling anywhere from 5 to 15 percent and a decent tip in the neighbourhood of 15 percent, customers know they will pay up to 30 percent too much for their food as soon as they set foot in the restaurant.

In a more high-end restaurant, you also need to calculate a higher margin per plate. With sales made mainly Thursday to Saturday evening, you need a big margin just to break even.

A plate of pasta with rosé sauce that costs $15 before tax can cost less than $3 to cook at home. The more the restaurant relies on volume, the thinner the margin per plate; the more the restaurant relies on differentiation (fancy decor, space between tables, refined cuisine, and so on), the higher the margin per plate.

How much would a $150 dinner at a restaurant cost to prepare at home? Conservatively, probably less than half. And that's just a single meal.

Television shows about cooking, kitchen renovation, and amateur and professional chef competitions are more popular than ever. But we have probably never cooked so little, and the number of restaurants is growing.

It's amusing to see delivery people ring the doorbell at a house with a kitchen worth $50,000 or more. It would be enough to make my grandfather Anatole's hair stand on end. On Friday evenings he would go to the grocery store to buy items that had been marked down, as they were close to their expiration date.

Food courts

The food courts of yesteryear have changed a lot. In shopping malls, fast-food chains proliferate. This sort of restaurant essentially wipes out the nutritional value of the food we eat. Salt, sugar, fat and starch are what's on offer.

In food courts, it looks as though there is competition, but in fact many of the franchise banners are owned by the same group. Take the MTY Group, listed on the Toronto Stock Exchange.

They are the mother ship to a number of well-known banners, including Cultures, KimChi, Thai Express, Tandori, Muffin Plus, Tiki-Ming, Mucho Burrito, Vie & Nam, Café Dépôt, Sushi Shop, Franx Supreme, Valentine, Tutti Frutti and Madisons. In other words, you will often find yourself in a food court where everything on offer is from a single group.

At the food court, when you pay $10 for a meal, the shopping centre, franchisee and franchisor all take their cut. So it is economically unrealistic to believe there's nutritional value in what you are eating. If you pay $10, you get what you pay for, which is to say almost nothing.

When I worked at McDonald's in 1996, the owner told me that the cup cost about the same as the liquid it contained: a few cents. That meant he could afford to offer free refills on drinks.

The idea of the fast-food combo is an unusual marketing strategy. If you buy only a sandwich, it costs practically the same as a combo. For a little extra, you get the "cup of liquid sugar" and "fries with no potatoes" served with the sandwich. But that little extra adds up to a lot for the merchant when multiplied order after order.

With or without tax?
Sales tax is a specific field of taxation. It's a complex subject with many exceptions. But as a consumer, it is a good idea to have another perspective on consumption. For example, certain basic necessities aren't taxable, such as meat, fruit, vegetables, fish and milk.

But if these foods are heated to consume, they are technically taxable. So if a caterer offers you a hot dish that is ready to eat, it is taxable. On the other hand, if it is packaged and put in the fridge and cools down, it is non-taxable, because you have to heat it up at home (taxation can get pretty arcane).

If you buy a carton of milk at the corner store, it isn't taxable, but if you buy it from a vending machine, it may be. If you buy a single pastry, there is sales tax, but if you buy six, that's a different story and they aren't taxable. It all tastes the same, but the larger format affects the price.

As a result, when you go to the bakery, it's better to buy six croissants than five. But who is really interested in the sales tax applied to their purchases? No one.

Quantities

At restaurants, to make a profit, chefs tend to pile starch on the plate. It's cheaper. At home, you would probably eat less. At restaurants, you don't tend to notice that there is less of the more expensive food on your plate.

For example, with sushi, if you separated out all the protein, you would notice that there is a minimal amount on a $7 five-piece plate. Another important thing to remember is that, at home, you benefit from economies of scale: you can make four servings but eat just one. You serve more reasonable portions and don't feel bad putting the leftovers in the fridge for lunch the next day.

Time

For most meals, cooking doesn't take that much time, but it does take planning. That's the point at which things often break down. We neglect to plan because of our busy schedules. Then suddenly we are hungry and don't know what to make. And bam! We grab the phone and order a brown chicken, brown fries, brown sauce and beige coleslaw for delivery. We tip for a meal that arrives soggy from condensation and thermal shock. We finish the meal stuffed, telling ourselves we need to change our ways, until the next time.

Cooking is the activity that we should subcontract the least. Personally, it's my Achilles heel. This is one area where I should do more to walk the talk.

FREE TIPS!

Have tomato sauce parties! No time to cook? Don't enjoy it? That's understandable, but with wine and some friends, it can be fun. On a Saturday, make sauce with a group of friends and eat pasta together that evening. Afterwards, everyone can take home the leftover portions to refrigerate or freeze.

It's important to eat vegetables, but they can be quite expensive. Watch the frozen food aisle. Several times a year, Canadian vegetables are much cheaper than fresh vegetables from Chile or Argentina. Save your money and the planet!

Cooking for yourself means controlling the timing, quantity, quality and nutritional value of food. So, economically speaking, you really need it. Now you just have to decide who'll do the dishes . . .

A TIE
DO YOU REALLY NEED IT?

I t needs to be said: neckties are silly. Whether you pay $10, $40, $80 or $120 for one, its role is dubious at best. Ties are worn out of conformity and to look "professional."

In reality, ties are just bits of hanging fabric. An arrow pointing to the centre of the male universe: the penis. But they make the most precious asset—the head—uncomfortable. Like lawyers' bands, they are part of a dress code adopted long ago that is perpetuated out of convention. We need to shout it from the rooftops: "Enough is enough!"

One day, seeing the pile of fabric arrows pointing at my pants and gathering dust in the closet, I gathered most of the ties I had collected over the years, put them in a bag and donated them to the Salvation Army.

Of course, men are willing to wear ties for certain social occasions, such as weddings, company functions and awards ceremonies. But even then, we do so reluctantly. **Honestly, who likes walking around with a noose around their neck?** Whether simple, four-in-hand, half-Windsor or Windsor, it's still a knot. A scout badge should be awarded for every one mastered.

Are ties necessary?

Ties are **like a thong in your crack: they may look good, but they're uncomfortable.** (I merely hypothesize, for the sake of comparison. I would have to do a survey of women to confirm it.) The proof is that, when men wear a tie, the first thing they do the minute they can is loosen it or take it off. It's suffocating; it presses on you; it restricts your breathing. The shirt collar cries out for air, and the top button seems to be saying, "Are you really doing me up?"

Ties are corsets for men. But in no way do they improve a man's shape. In fact, doing up the top button can make excess skin bulge over the collar.

When I worked at McDonald's, the cooks had to constantly get their ties out of the way by flipping them over their shoulders. It's okay to want to be professional, but having your tie dangle in mustard and hamburger grease isn't just unhygienic; it's revolting.

Ties were clearly made for an antiseptic workplace. If your tie gets caught in a running motor, it's strangulation guaranteed. Wearing a tie says to your attacker, "Go ahead and strangle me!" Like a reverse hanging, it is practically a sign of the servitude of the average worker. It's a metaphor of the employer-employee relationship, with the more powerful of the two saying, "I've got you by the throat."

A short history of fashion

Fashion cycles render ties completely absurd. Once you have a selection of wide ties, skinny ties come back into style. When you get skinny ones, medium-width ties make a comeback. Bright colours the thing? The following year, ties will be pale and drab.

One year contrast is in, and the next year it's tone on tone. After a few years, any self-respecting professional finds himself with a collection of pieces of fabric, the only thing special about them being their complete lack of utility, even though some pieces in the collection would make any clothes horse jealous.

Constantly updating your wardrobe of ties is akin to starting a fire with $100 bills: it's an unwise investment. One underestimated aspect of the tie is its discrimination. Unbeknownst to them, men with short necks suffer from the image their ties create: it's as if someone has hit them on the head with a mallet, like in a Whac-a-Mole game. Why not release them from their suffocation? Why not let their necks see the sun?

People may say, "Yes, but it's like jewellery. It enhances your appearance." But while the tie is an accepted convention, the comparison doesn't hold up, since a beautiful necklace doesn't compromise neck comfort.

I would like to know what we gain by wearing ties. When business casual came on the professional scene, ties started to go out the window. **To be productive, we need to declare war on discomfort.** I want the right to look professional without a tie. I want to be free of all the knotted nonsense. I want the right not to have a budget just for ties.

EATING YOUR SOCKS
DO YOU REALLY NEED TO?

When it comes to personal finance, spending isn't the only thing you need to control. You need to learn to manage your income and professional market value. Do you want to be a unique product with significant added value, or would you rather eat your socks? Sometimes, people eat so many socks to get a contract or a job that their breath starts to smell like a wool-cotton blend.

To tap into an opportunity or find their niche, people often settle for eating their socks, even without a little ketchup. In other words, they sell themselves for less than they should.

To make your mark and prove your worth, sometimes you have to offer a strategic discount. But if you keep that up, you end up being seen as a low-end product that can be exploited. In marketing, when you sell a product or service for a low price, you are banking on volume, not margin. The problem with volume when selling your time is that you end up working more hours for less money.

In French, *manger ses bas* literally means "to eat your socks." Figuratively, it's a Québécois expression for selling yourself short. You'll see what I mean.

A good example is the freelance print journalist. To publish, some writers agree to research and write an article for as little as $50, or even less than minimum wage. When you earn less per hour writing an article[1] than flipping burgers at McDonald's, it may be time to set your base rate, even if it means losing contracts. You need to set a minimum rate at the beginning of your career. That rate becomes your anchoring bias (see "Negotiating: Do You Really Need It?" on page 32) in negotiations with future clients.

Textile manufacturers love sock eaters. As long as you keep swallowing, they keep the looms operating. **Eventually, the day will come when you get indigestion and need to put your foot down: you can't work for peanuts.** The only way to stop eating cotton is to create your professional market value. You need to ask yourself:

- What differentiates me?
- Why would someone pay me more than someone else?
- Am I faster, more talented, more reliable, more available, nicer, more understanding or more flexible?
- Do I have expertise that is scarce to the point of being irreplaceable?

If you can't identify your added value, how can a potential employer? Offering your labour at a discount can't be the only thing that differentiates you. If it is, you will become a professional sock eater: someone who sows a lot but reaps little. The more you munch on your socks, the more the quality of the fibre deteriorates: from cotton and wool, you end up with Phentex.

You also need to know your market.

---

1   For instance, as an unpaid blogger for a media company.

- How many sock eaters are there in my field?
- How many people are prepared to work harder than me, at a lower rate?
- Which of them are ingesting so much wool, they are literally swallowing the sheep whole?

And while you're at it, you should be asking other questions:

- Am I a sock eater in the making?
- Does my field of study allow me to kick back and relax?
- Am I in a specialized field where expertise is scarce?
- In looking at placement statistics for graduates, is the heading "future sock eater" implicitly part of the job description?

Some people experience a rude awakening after they graduate. After getting a bachelor's or master's degree in sock eating, they complain that their salary is pathetic or too low given their education. But, as we know, a master's in polyester chomping leads directly to long-term sock ingestion.

Non–sock eaters can vote with their feet: they can quit their job or turn down contracts. If someone is allergic to textile fibre or if they aren't satisfied with their lot, they can offer their services elsewhere. But just because you leave one sock manufacturer doesn't mean you won't be stuck in a market filled with similar manufacturers.

Before you gag, you should be asking yourself whether or not you are in a position to demand that you earn a certain living. **But regardless, eating your socks puts wear and tear on your jaw and dries up happiness.** So before agreeing to another contract at a cut rate, you may need to ask yourself whether you really need yet another low-paying job. If you do, you need to get used to being in stocking feet.

There are two sorts of sock eaters:
employees and self-employed workers.

Sock-eating employee

Self-employed sock eater

THE EMPLOYEE

This is the traditional sock eater. The employee works hard, knitting away in her corner, and ends up carving out a place for herself. She gets her first job because of good marks in school or an impressive resumé, one that is more finely woven than those of her classmates.

A lucky combination of both is obviously a better guarantee of success. Her starting salary and how she navigates her career will determine her salary growth.

She will fight her entire career to have her value recognized and keep her salary competitive. The starting salary in a job is the sinews of war.

Sometimes, you need to move to another organization to catch up on your salary or enjoy competitive conditions. Employees are combatants in negotiations (see "Negotiating: Do You Really Need It?" on page 32). If they don't fight the fight, they are destined to choke on their sock wool, at a low price.

THE SELF-EMPLOYED WORKER

Compensation for self-employed workers tends to mirror a company's life cycle.

Introductory phase – The self-employed worker, at this point unknown, offers his services. There are two strategies. The first is to offer a price that beats the competition, while benefiting from volume and, as a result, eating his socks.

The second is to offer a differentiator so he can negotiate a higher rate. Despite his lack of experience, the self-employed worker tries to find a distinctive value: the quality of his work, a scarce skill, a differentiated product or service, a fast turnaround, ancillary services, and so on.

Growth phase – The self-employed worker is becoming established. His name is making the rounds, and he is investing in his company to make it grow. He starts investing in capital assets as needed, but liquidity is still a major challenge. This is the point at which he needs to raise his rates: his visibility is slowly building, and offers for contracts are coming in. He needs to show discernment in choosing contracts, while trying to build customer loyalty.

Maturity phase – The self-employed worker is no longer eating socks at this stage, because he has established his credibility. He has achieved his maximum price. He coasts on the reputation that has been built during the growth years. He maintains his service offer. If he is still eating socks at this point, it is because he enjoys being taken advantage of, or the quality of his services does not justify higher rates than those of his competitors.

Decline phase – In pre-retirement, the self-employed worker may not be as available, be as driven in his work or have the same adaptability as newcomers to the market. There will always be people who are younger and crazier waiting in the wings.

Whether you are self-employed or an employee, you need to demonstrate your distinctive value. When it comes to personal finance, the key is not only managing expenses but intelligently managing income as well. Negotiating your fair market value is an art. Put yourself in the place of a client or employer, and ask why you would pay that price.

What is your distinctive value? If nothing comes to mind, I hope you like wool or polyester. Do you REALLY want to eat socks your whole life?

If the answer is no, what are you doing to stop digesting fibre? You need to pick a side: I choose the side of non-sock eaters.

A HAIR SALON
DO YOU REALLY NEED IT?

I can see you leaping out of your chair: "This time, McSween, you've gone too far!"

The topic of this chapter is somewhat arbitrary. I could have used plenty of other expense categories. **But hair salons are a fascinating place to see the discrepancy between the value of the service rendered and the end result.**

The other thing that is fascinating is how they have transformed over time. What was once a simple haircut has become a long and involved experience. And an expensive one.

Another era

When I was little, I went to the barber's. The experience was pretty basic: a chair, a comb, a razor, and in ten or fifteen minutes, Bob was your uncle. No appointment necessary. It was something nice I did with my dad every couple of months.[1] We spent $7 to get our hair cut, the barber gave me a 2-cent cherry

---

1 Barbershops still exist. Shout-out to Ménick Barber Shop on rue Masson in Montreal.

gumball, and I would leave content. It was a time of lazy Saturdays and stores that were closed on Sundays. You could enjoy the slow pace of the weekend and savour having nothing to do.

Hair dye

One day, hair dye marketing, which up until then had been mainly for women who were going grey, changed tack. Someone came up with the idea of telling young women that something was wrong with their natural colour, but there was an easy solution.

Bam! Sales increased. Women starting buying more hair dye at the drugstore and having their hair professionally coloured. Brunettes were told they should go blond and blondes should become redheads. And the money poured in.

Then the pace got ramped up. On top of worrying about the length of their hair and maintaining their ends, people also had to think about their roots, increasing the amount of money spent and guaranteeing a loyal clientele. Some women have never even considered taking a break from dying their hair regularly.

Why would you dye your hair when you are at your most beautiful? Why stress out your follicles when you're young and have a perfectly fine natural colour?

Because marketing demands it. And when marketing wants something, it convinces you to want it too. It will convince you that your natural hair isn't shiny. It can even convince you to dye your hair when you like your natural colour. Go on, get on that!

The customer experience

At some point, dying and styling were no longer enough. How do they justify price hikes? Ah yes: the fashionable decor. Salons started offering specialty coffees, then cocktails. They even created a sort of social hierarchy: stylist, colourist and the person who washes your hair. And all of them need a tip.

Eventually, a simple haircut had become a day of beauty care, with the correspondingly steep price tag. Over the course of a year, a woman who dyes her hair every month, at $100 a shot, will have spent $1,200 of her net pay on her hair. It's pretty crazy when you think about it.

The pink tax

The most nonsensical aspect of salons is the price, which is different for men and women.

At one time, when I had hair down to my shoulders, a woman showed up at a salon with hair shorter than mine, but she still paid more than me. Why? Does service for women, on average, require more treatments or more time than for men?

I was going to get my ends trimmed, like plenty of women do. She paid more, even though she too was only getting a trim. The price was based on sex rather than the effort involved. It's a bit like young men paying more for car insurance. Victims of statistical discrimination? That's one explanation, but the answer probably lies more in the frequency of service.

I think the different price structure is more a matter of competition. Barbers and hair salons for men where you don't need an appointment offer customers an inexpensive service. That means that men have a cheaper option than fashionable salons with their higher prices.

Even in his-and-hers salons, men don't pay as much as women. For the average man, the impression of receiving a value-added service doesn't justify a higher price. Given that most men have their hair cut more often and that the services at a barber are delivered faster, the price of a haircut for men is based on the number of visits (volume) and not on a differentiated service.

Something else explains the difference as well: anchoring bias (see "Negotiating: Do You Really Need It?" on page 32). Women are used to paying more for the services they receive at salons, so why drop the price if they are prepared to pay it?

Price sends a signal: the higher it is, the more it means luxury. When you choose a fashionable salon with an impressive decor and five-star service, it needs to be reflected in the price.

A familiar growth strategy

When a business model has become stagnant, the powers that be try to increase the revenue it generates. They try to figure out a growth strategy. The hair salon and cosmetics industry have understood this. For example:

- ✔ You can develop a new product in an existing market (a new anti-aging cream).
- ✔ You can sell an existing product in a new market (the first to sell dye to young women).
- ✔ You can diversify by selling a new product or service in a new market (as Nivea did by creating cream for men— see below).
- ✔ Or you can sell an existing product in an existing market: you need to compete on price to penetrate this market.

WHAT ABOUT BEAUTY PRODUCTS?

While I was doing my bachelor's degree at HEC Montréal, companies would use us to do market studies for their new products, asking us to taste or test them.

One day, I received a sample of Nivea Men cream. I thought, "This will never take off. It's probably the same product as for women, but with the word *Men* written on the tube."

I was wrong to discount it. I mean, why pass up 50 percent of your potential clientele? And in fact, products for men have exploded on the cosmetics market. By signalling to men on the packaging that the product is for them, their masculinity remains intact.

You know what? My bathroom shelf has face cream for men (your face can get a little chapped in winter). It's become part of my daily routine.

Beauty marketing gets into our heads and finds a corner in which to lodge its ideas. It creates desire. Or does it awaken dormant desires? This is an endless debate that keeps management schools going. Regardless, the recipe works, so it is applied, just like face cream.

So, a hair salon where a haircut costs $100: do you really need it? Seriously? Every month? Every other month?

"Listen, McSween, I can do what I want with my money!"

"You're right. How's your RRSP doing? You can't afford one? Oh, I see. Of course, you're right. Do what you want with your money. *Carpe diem!*"

PREPARING FOR FAILURE
DO YOU REALLY NEED TO?

Lots of people base their personal financial planning on a false premise: that things will always go well. Obviously, you need to have a positive approach to life. And you may indeed be lucky. But the head is a strange beast: it can lead us into incredible adventures or make us lose our way.

When it comes to personal finance, you need to prepare for failure. Failure at what? Therein lies the question. Failure is personal and comes in different degrees of intensity. For some people, life will take a murky detour. That's not cynical. That's statistical.

Making decisions today for tomorrow

In our society, we need to make long-term decisions based on the information we have today. Average workers look at the pay deposited to their account and spend based on that amount. They take out a mortgage, move into the house and pay their bills. As long as everything balances every month, they keep on smiling as they open a can of Molson Ex bought on sale at Costco.

Then life changes. Quickly, suddenly, with no warning.

Our chances of messing things up in life are both high and unpredictable. **It takes years to cook up a life that tastes good, but it only takes an instant to have it turn bitter.** Financially, you need a bit of leeway to deal with the unexpected failure waiting just around the corner.

Crossing a busy boulevard, Isabelle is hit by a car. She'll spend the next eighteen months in rehab.

Mathieu goes on a surfing vacation—and comes home in a wheelchair.

Out of the blue, Annie's marriage ends. She loses her grip and can't go back to work.

Yesterday's error wipes out today's good times.

Martin wakes up with a pain in his stomach. His doctor gives him a diagnosis that includes the word *terminal*.

A lapse of judgment changes a peaceful life into hell.

A moment of inattention at the wheel causes irreparable damage.

Crying on the inside

Every day, you come across people in the street who are crying. You don't see their tears, because they are crying on the inside. Even if they wear a smile as a mask, their mind is not at peace. Too much pain, a ruined future, a load so heavy to carry that, as soon as they wake up, dark thoughts take over.

Seeing people around them smiling only deepens their sadness: the gap between other people's happiness and their own situation is too great. Sometimes, they look at a beam in their living room and think that a hook and a rope would put an end to their unhappiness.

There are failures you never come back from, that are so painful you can't face up to them. A failure that necrotizes daily life with the associated guilt.

Guilt is like rust. It starts by leaving a mark. Slowly, it attacks the whole body, then the engine (the head), and disrupts your ability to function. The machine collapses and can't handle everyday tasks. Everything is a mountain to climb, and morale is at its lowest ebb.

When these situations strike, a lack of financial resources is a trap that can lead straight to the abyss. You need to protect yourself against life's problems by having insurance, financial leeway (see "Financial Leeway: Do You Really Need It?" on page 1) or considerable assets. That way, you might be able to get out of your tight spot rather than getting wedged in it.

What if . . .

. . . that instant had been different? What would have happened next? If, in that very moment, I had chosen the other option, made that other choice?

When you think about it:

80 years in life is . . .
29,220 days . . .
701,280 hours . . .
42,076,800 minutes . . .
2,524,608,000 seconds.

All it takes is a fraction of a second to change the course of a life. When what follows that second is positive, you don't think about it anymore. But when a negative event compromises your future happiness, the mind can't take it. People will tell you that you just need to come to terms with things. They urge you to accept the darker side of chance, even though you know that chance is a series of factors you only partially control.

Others will tell you that it was just circumstance. When you think about it, it's hard to fathom how we can come out unscathed at the end of the road. We encounter so many obstacles along the way, and it is quite likely that one of them becomes insurmountable.

All that time working to build something, for nothing. All that time spent thinking about tomorrow, only to end up living as if it were yesterday. That is the irony of our lives, dotted with false successes and real failures (or real successes and false failures). It's all a matter of perception.

Despite it all, there is that moment, that parenthesis, that comma in one's existence that, combined with seconds, becomes the fateful moment that sets the tone for everything to follow.

Being floored

Near my house, there is a building managed by an organization that helps people who have been knocked down by life and who never managed to get up again. These people live on social assistance and pay reduced rent. They used to live somewhere else before life dealt them a blow.

Sometimes I think about the circumstances that brought them to the breaking point. I wonder whether I would be able to survive that sort of failure. Financially, could I get back up off the ground a year or two after a failure? **What is my financial plan if life's referee decides to toss me out of the game?**

You need to be able to answer these questions. Whether it is disability insurance or selling assets, you need a financial crutch to get back on your feet.

Grief: a daily vaccine

Grief is like a vaccine: we administer it in small doses, until eventually we experience the ultimate grief—grieving our own life. These moments of life go by fairly sequentially: grieving childhood, innocence, school, a carefree life, first love, family life, active life, the range of possibilities, new experiences, travel, health, your mind, then your whole life. **When facing sudden misfortune, you need to grieve certain things: perfection and life as you knew it.**

Failure and grieving are intimately linked: you can't have one without the other. Society doesn't prepare you for misfortune; it drives people to succeed. So when tragedy strikes, you don't always have the strength to deal with it. You need to protect yourself against the day when the oak can no longer withstand the storm. Against the day when someone finds you in the fetal position crying in the shower.

No one is immune to depression or a senseless accident. Do you really need to prepare for failure? It's hard to generalize, because you may not be in control of how you react.

BANKRUPTCY
DO YOU REALLY NEED IT?

I'll come right out and say it: declaring bankruptcy isn't the end of the world. Bankruptcy definitely has a major impact on your credit rating and on access to credit for a few years. But is it as bad as all that? Bankruptcy exists to give people a second chance. It's a legal procedure that gives everyone room to fail.

Bankruptcy isn't always the result of poor management; it may be the tragic end to bad luck in business or an idea that just didn't take off. When you have a dream and you go all in, sometimes things don't work out. Sometimes the real failure isn't declaring bankruptcy, but not doing it at the right time.

When do you need to declare bankruptcy?

A management professor who had ups and downs in his entrepreneurial life, going from growing a small business to managing a Quebec Inc. company through to the bankruptcy of some of his companies, had this to say in class: "Declaring personal or business bankruptcy isn't the end of the world. The important thing is to choose to declare bankruptcy before others choose it for you."

As in theatre, you have to stage even your failure. You have to see it like an event in life, one among others. It's like pressing the reset button on a Nintendo console in the 1980s: you lose everything you accumulated during the game and have to start over. Everything? Not really. **There's one good thing about bankruptcy: it has rules that offer minimal protection for people who lose almost everything.**

It is important to point out that you need to consult a trustee in bankruptcy if you think your financial situation has got out of hand.[1] Before you end up in bankruptcy, there may be other solutions to explore.

A deep breath in, a deep breath out

The first thing to do is to take a deep breath in and let it out. If you are reading this and your financial situation is keeping you up at night, you need to calm down. Money is just a game. Yes, it's a game that has a major impact on our lives. Some people play their cards better than others or are just luckier when they roll the dice.

When you lose at the game of life or are in a vulnerable situation, it is important to come up with a strategy. Rather than keep rolling the dice, it's best to consult an expert to get an overview of the situation.

In my role as a radio show commentator, I remember getting e-mails from listeners who were panicking because they didn't know what to do about their disastrous financial situation. One of them wrote to tell me he was losing sleep because he couldn't

---

1   To find out more about the topic, I suggest visiting https://bankruptcycanada.com/bankruptcy-law-3/.

pay his credit card balance, and he didn't want his spouse to have to pay off his debts.

Unfortunately, by default spouses are along for the ride. If one spouse can't make ends meet, that affects vacation plans, nights out and lifestyle choices for the whole household. You need to talk things over and come up with the best solution for both people. Definitely, the first thing you need to do is cut up your credit cards and start paying for things with cash or debit.

> **But I'll stop earning any points!**

> **Oh, for god's sake!**

(See "!%#*?& Points Cards: Do You Really Need Them?" on page 49.)

Using your credit card to accumulate points is like collecting bottles to supplement your income: the return is extremely limited.

Solutions for getting out of debt

Before the final step of bankruptcy, there are a few basic tricks to get rid of consumer debt. First off, if you have a credit card with an interest rate of 19.99 percent, why not apply for a line of credit?

The interest rate on a line of credit is often less than half that on a credit card. If, one month, you can't pay the balance on your credit card, you can always pay it off with your line of credit at a lower rate.

If you have capital in your house and have run up a major debt (for example, $30,000), you can consider remortgaging your house to come up with the capital. It isn't free, but if it can stop a couple from getting further in the hole, it's worth considering. The cost of a mortgage loan is low because of the collateral in the form of the house, so this is a potential solution.

Here are other possible avenues:

- ✔ **Consolidating your debt**: This is the solution if you have many debts, some with a high interest rate. A financial institution can grant you a loan to pay off your debts.

  Then you make a single monthly payment. But you need to consider debt consolidation early in the game: once your credit rating is seriously blemished, financial institutions may not grant the loan.
- ✔ **Negotiating with your creditors**: Sometimes creditors prefer to relax their terms rather than not be paid at all. You can ask your creditors to change the payment time frame, the amount of the payments and sometimes even the interest rate. Even if you owe on your income tax, you can try to strike an agreement with the Canada Revenue Agency to spread the payments out over several months. Nothing is forcing your creditors to change the terms of the loan, but it can't hurt to ask. Nothing ventured, nothing gained.
- ✔ **Voluntary deposit:** To avoid bankruptcy, you may decide on voluntary deposit. This is a procedure that has you turn over part of your salary to the Court. Creditors receive a payment based on the deposit. The advantage of this solution is that it lets you pay a reasonable interest

rate on your debt. It is something worth considering before your salary is garnisheed.

✔ **Consumer proposal:** With the help of a trustee in bankruptcy, you make a proposal to creditors about all of your debt (not including your mortgage). This allows you to reduce your total debt if the creditors agree. They are not obliged to do so, but they may question whether they will get more of their money back by forcing you into bankruptcy or by accepting your proposal.

For the person who is in debt, a consumer proposal stops the accumulation of interest and collection efforts by creditors. But it will appear on the person's credit history.

Bankruptcy

Bankruptcy isn't a magical solution to get out of debt. It's not free. You need to wave goodbye to certain assets and pay. To go bankrupt, you have to have debt of at least $1,000 and be judged to be in difficult financial straits. For example, the value of all of your property must be less than the debt.

Even if you are in a position of bankruptcy, you need to pay the trustee in bankruptcy and sometimes even "discharge" yourself from bankruptcy through payments spread over a certain amount of time and calculated based on your ability to pay.

A number of types of debt can be funnelled into the bankruptcy (personal loans, credit cards, lines of credit and more). Other debt is excluded, such as debt for spousal support and fraud, as well as some student loans (depending on how much time has passed since the person ended his or her studies).

Some property is protected from bankruptcy, particularly a portion of those items related to basic needs: clothing, food, work tools and more.

You are generally discharged from bankruptcy after nine months.[1] For a first bankruptcy, a note generally appears in your credit file for six years after the date of the discharge.[2]

Another good reason to contribute to an RRSP

Contrary to what some people believe, bankruptcy has no impact on your retirement savings: neither an employer plan nor an RRSP (except the last twelve months' contributions) can be seized. Why aren't contributions from the past year protected?

 To ensure that someone who is planning on bankruptcy doesn't make huge contributions to an RRSP with the most recent money borrowed.

Getting back on your feet

It bears repeating: losing everything isn't the end of the world. If you think your family and children won't be able to make a change in lifestyle, think again. People are extraordinarily resilient. Is everyone healthy? That's the main thing.

In the game of money, you can start over. Obviously, it won't be all that great, but the important thing is to have quickly spotted the need to make a new start. You have to take the hit and learn how to laugh about it. **There is no shame in losing everything.**

---

1   https://bankruptcy-canada.com/how-to-file-bankruptcy-canada/bankruptcy-discharge/

2   https://bankruptcy-canada.com/bankruptcy-blog/bankruptcy-affect-credit-rating/

When we see people stumble, our collective admiration often goes out to those who have the guts to get back up. Do you remember athletes who won a medal at the 1992 Olympics? Mark Tewksbury, Sylvie Fréchette, Linford Christie, Mike Powell, Carl Lewis and Boris Becker might come to mind.

But there was also a guy named Derek Redmond whose story, a quarter of a century after he competed, continues to make the rounds of the Internet. Why? Because Derek Redmond failed courageously.

After an injury obliterated his Olympic dream, he got back on his feet and ended his race crying and limping, to a standing ovation from the tens of thousands of spectators in the stadium. The spectators will be able to say for the rest of their lives, "I was there."

Yes, we admire winners, but we admire those who lift themselves back up even more. Talking about your financial failure may help those around you feel less alone. Then one day, when they stumble, they will have the courage to get back on their feet, thinking of you, the Derek Redmond in their lives.

NB: The information in this chapter is incomplete and summary. It is provided to plant a seed in the minds of readers and offer them solutions before they get to the last step: bankruptcy.

It is important to find a solution that suits you. This is why it is necessary to consult a professional who will be able to determine the best option before you make any decisions.

Financial problems are part of life. You can't plan for or be protected from everything, not even from your own mistakes. For there to be winners in the money game, there need to be losers.

Bankruptcy: do you really need it? Maybe. The important thing is to be aware of it if you do, and to recognize that it's not the end of the world.[1]

---

1   I'm not questioning how serious bankruptcy is. It's not ideal, but as my godfather, Richard McSween, says, "There are worse things in life."

PLANNING FOR YOUR DEATH
DO YOU REALLY NEED TO?

At a dinner, a family friend I've known since childhood (she'd changed my diapers) told us that she was worried about the expenses that would be generated by her death. She didn't want to leave this financial burden to her children and, as a result, she was thinking of donating her body to science.

We chatted about other options, such as a mass grave, a cardboard box, cut-rate cremation or a plywood urn. At that point, my father and I started to have some fun with it. We came up with a business plan: We would jerry-rig caskets on the cheap, using recycled and recovered materials. Everything would be made in a co-operative with the mission of helping young, unemployed people reintegrate into society.

It was a great concept with a community calling. We would even offer people the option to make their own coffin with loving care. And why not let loved ones write on the casket? Why varnish wood that will just end up underground anyway?

Our plan even included saving churches in Quebec, because their unused basements and presbyteries would become showrooms that we would rent. Basically, for some of the services delivered, we would bypass the death industry entirely.

Of course, we were just goofing around, but we had realized something: **an inexpensive death is possible, but frowned upon.** Which raises the question: why devote so much of our financial resources to our death when we could have made use of that money to live out our final days in a better fashion?

The guarantee

In some ways, the marketing of death is odd. For example, we seal the coffin to preserve the body longer. Great! But who digs up a body to make sure it's preserved? In rare cases, it's true, the deceased's DNA needs to be checked (as with a recent paternity claim related to Salvador Dali, for instance).

Sometimes salespeople offer copper casing for the casket, to protect the body even more and make people shell out cash for no reason. Why is there this obsession with preserving the body? We will all be eaten by worms. No matter what the budget, the worms devour us in the end. All of us.

There are people who freeze their bodies to preserve them until they can be brought back to life. The type of person who took the legend of Walt Disney too seriously or, perhaps, saw the movie *Vanilla Sky*.

Life's great equalizer is that we will all die. So why try to inject luxury into the final chapter of our life? **Isn't dying in simplicity the ultimate lesson in humility?** Why use all those materials that won't decompose? Why contaminate the soil? If people could live forever, we would run out of space. Why try to preserve a body below or above ground?

Dying is like saying, "My turn is up. I had happiness, felt

sadness, enjoyed a range of experiences, but it's my time to
go." Our last lap may come prematurely, but we know that
we all die; we just think it comes too soon.

So why pay to leave a trace of yourself for all eternity,
when no one will remember you? We are all destined to be for-
gotten; why not come to terms with that for not too much money?
Some people want gilded funerals, while others prefer to leave
what they have to their loved ones, or enjoy it themselves while
they're still alive.

The Canada Pension Plan to the rescue!
Are you getting on in years and haven't put aside minimal finan-
cial resources for your burial? No problem. The Canada Pension
Plan (CPP) could make a final, posthumous payment to you.

Contributing to the CPP during your working life not only
provides you a basic pension, it also allows the future deceased
(which is to say, all of us) to receive a maximum death benefit of
$2,500. (In Quebec, equivalent benefits are available from the
Quebec Pension Plan [QPP].) Check out the respective websites
for details on how much could be available to your relatives who
must cover your funeral expenses.

The death benefit is taxable as estate income, regardless of
who receives it, because it was used for the deceased. The information is incomplete at this point, but the message is: ask and
you may receive!

Options for death
Nothing is free here on earth. An entire book could be written
on the death industry, the cost analysis, prearrangements and so
on. This chapter is more a reflection on the resources we put

toward death. I'll toss out a bit of economically rational food for thought.

A cardboard coffin

 Why not just buy a cardboard coffin? It's much cheaper, and since burial or cremation are not a long-term investment, do you really need to waste valuable raw materials?

A biodegradable urn

It's fun to see urns that look like works of art. Yet they end up underground. Why put ashes in a beautiful wooden box or an expensive metal container? Why not use a reusable decorative box during the funeral service that the real biodegradable urn can be placed in? Makes sense, doesn't it?

For people who pay to keep the ashes in a columbarium, is the ability for visitors to be physically close to the ashes so important? They can always be put in the ground. The advantage of burying ashes is that the hole costs much less to dig than the hole for a coffin, and the family can carry the remains of their loved one rather than the funeral home staff (everything is billed piecemeal in funeral homes).

Become a tree

After a cremation, you can do what you want with the ashes. Why not spread them in the forest or plant a tree from them, in a locale that had meaning for the deceased? On top of being a symbol for the survivors, the tree will limit the environmental footprint and costs related to the death.

Express cremation

While some funeral homes specialize in high-end, varied services, others specialize in low-cost packages. Here is the basic funeral service:

- ✔ *Transporting the body.* You don't want to have to call your brother-in-law to bring his pickup truck or minivan to get the body from the morgue to the crematorium.
- ✔ *Cremation expenses.* Because you can't make a campfire in the backyard, even if you're a Darth Vader fan.
- ✔ *Legal formalities.* Because you have to register the death.

Once the body has been turned to ashes, you don't need to pay the funeral home for transporting them; a friend can do it. You can even find people who offer this service for less: they transport the ashes from a crematorium far from where you live to the desired location.

Obviously, it's then a matter of the choice of urn and how the ashes will be handled. If you have decided to bury them and you have rights on a plot in a cemetery, you still have to pay to have the hole dug, even though it is shallow. Some people prefer to keep the deceased's ashes in the living room at home. Everyone has their own feelings on this.

Other expenses

Online funeral service providers will bill you for a wide range of fees,[1] including:

---

1   Fees may vary.

- ✔ Transporting the ashes to the cemetery: $125
- ✔ Chapel rental: $500
- ✔ Funeral service adviser: $250
- ✔ Officiant's honorarium: $200

You will also be offered online services, such as a commemorative site that will be up for a few years. And while you're at it, why not purchase carbon credits to be carbon neutral when you die? Or why not have a commemorative video of your life produced for an additional sum? There is no end to death-related services.

Why make final arrangements?

Why is it important, financially speaking, to make arrangements for your death? First, so that you don't leave your descendants with a big bill or force them to make major decisions in a moment of sadness (assuming that the people around you are fond of you, of course).

Then, and most importantly, to prevent your loved ones from falling for the folly of grandeur. **Expressing your final wishes prevents your heirs from feeling judged if they opt for a simple, affordable service.** Basically, you eliminate the fear of other people's judgment. Take the example of Michael Jackson's funeral, and do the opposite. A state funeral should not be the example for most of us mortals.

Besides, when you take into account the CPP/QPP death benefit, it is possible to die affordably. Dying shouldn't cost $10,000 or $20,000. Nor should we have to be tossed into a mass grave or donate our bodies to science to die for free.

So let's keep the crustless sandwiches and macaroni salad to a minimum. For this transition, what we need is for more people to avoid the traditional expense and bring a person's death down to its most basic: a final act of humility. From dust to dust.

NB: Obviously, one can also debate the importance of making a will and deciding on your beneficiaries. This topic is addressed in "Marriage: Do You Really Need It?" on page 100.

If estate planning isn't yet on your radar and you have children, stop reading right now and call a notary. It's urgent! Dying without a marriage contract or will and leaving behind minor children is an administrative and legal nightmare for the survivors.

Everything may not be settled according to your wishes. In terms of income tax, have no fear, because even when you die, someone will have to file at least one last tax return on your behalf. Life is taxable, even once you're dead.

Is it normal that the most expensive part of our life is the one that happens when we're dead? Whether your funeral costs $10,000 or $50,000, you are no less dead.

In the end, the only thing that truly counts is donating your organs. It's the truest way of giving of yourself.

A $20,000 funeral: do you really need it? Have you signed your medicare card? No, but you've thought of having your coffin sealed? Come on! The reality is that we should end our lives on earth in a simple, biodegradable brown paper bag.

CONCLUSION . . .
WHY DO YOU REALLY NEED IT?

Financial questions come up at every stage of our lives. The goal of this exercise on personal finance isn't to put you in a straitjacket of self-imposed simplicity or to advise you to be a cheapskate. What I want is to ask questions about how people use their financial resources.

The main goal of this book is to convince people aged fifteen to thirty-five to take their financial future in hand. The financial decisions they make during these two decades will mark the rest of their lives. But the book raises questions that will make people aged seven to seventy-seven think about their relationship with money.

By asking yourself the question "Do you really need it?"—and starting to ask it early in life—you raise further questions that will guide you in your spending choices.

- ✔ Am I really going to work one month out of the year just to buy this gadget?
- ✔ Am I the architect of my own misfortune?
- ✔ How much does not saving actually cost me?

- ✔ Am I thinking about my future and that of my children, or am I living as if life in a nursing home (which is not always fun) is just hypothetical?
- ✔ Am I truly free?
- ✔ Does not caring about money mean being a slave to monthly payments?

Asking yourself the question "Do I really need it?" before every purchase is also a way of putting yourself first, of giving yourself a boost.

Since time is our most valuable resource and it is limited, why spend your life paying for silly overspending? What drives us to spend so much? The answers to these critical questions are personal and require some soul-searching.

Saving is not an act of faith. It is a rational act. You will need the money you earn today tomorrow. Do you want to live like a modern-day slave or retain your freedom of choice? You need to allocate every dollar to a line on your budget where it will bring you the greatest happiness, not to mention your happiness for the next twenty years. What makes you happy?

Don't let this book sit on a shelf. Circulate it, lend it to your friends, leave it lying on a table at home or give it as a gift (even used). If readers get frustrated with me, I haven't achieved my goal. Frustrated readers may be the ones who write to financial columnists with messages like this:

> I'm at a loss. I'm forty years old, have no savings, and can't pay the balance on my credit card. I want to retire at fifty-eight. What should I do?

Here is my answer:

> Call Marty McFly, drive a DeLorean at 88 mph along the highway to travel twenty years into the past, and ask yourself this question: "Do you really need it?" If you don't really need it, but you keep driving your fancy car, I hope you like macaroni and Cheez Whiz.

Pierre-Yves McSween

ACKNOWLEDGEMENTS

Writing a book is great for the author, who gets to go to book fairs, but it takes a lot of help to get there. I would like to give special thanks to the following people, in no particular order.

CAROLINE LARRIVÉE, for everything you've done for our family.

PAUL-ANTOINE JETTÉ, for reading it, technical editing, your eagle eye, but most of all for your friendship.

PAUL ARCAND, for graciously agreeing to write the preface of a book by a columnist on your show *Puisqu'il faut se lever* and for having been, through a simple joke, the instigator of this project.

JEAN-FRANÇOIS ST-PIERRE, for your enthusiasm about the student you met for the first time at the Coop HEC Montréal.

JEAN PARÉ, for your enthusiasm for and openness to an impulsive, colourful accountant. Crazy ideas become realistic projects thanks to you.

ÉLISE BERGERON, for your work, discipline, overtime (even on the Fête Nationale), lending me an ear, your gentle nature, and acting as a buffer between me and the publishing world.

LOUISE SAUVÉ, YVES McSWEEN, ANNE-MARIE McSWEEN and MARIE-FRANCE McSWEEN, the family I would choose if given the chance.

DOMINIQUE LEROUX, according to whom we must follow our passions.

ÉDOUARD and ÉMILE, my sons, who give me two reasons to contribute to an RESP.

Thank you to the entire team at GUY SAINT-JEAN ÉDITEUR and their partners: your reception and support for this humble project are greatly appreciated.

Finally, thank you to YOU, the reader, who bought this book and who took the time to read it. To help you control your desire to spend, on the opposite page there's a sleeve for your credit card. Every time you want to book a flight online, buy an expensive purse or get the latest "must-have" item, your card will ask you, **"DO YOU REALLY NEED IT?"**

FOLD HERE

"DO YOU REALLY NEED IT?"

FOLD HERE

"DO YOU REALLY NEED IT?"

FOLD AND TAPE

CUT ALONG DOTTED LINE

1. CUT ALONG DOTTED LINE
2. FOLD ALONG SOLID LINE WHERE INDICATED
3. TAPE TOP EDGE AND ONE SIDE
4. SLIDE YOUR CREDIT CARD IN
5. FREE YOURSELF FINANCIALLY

PIERRE-YVES McSWEEN is a Fellow chartered professional accountant (MBA, FCPA, FCA), a business and economics columnist at FM 98.5 for two top-rated radio shows, and has written for *La Presse* and *Voir.ca*. He is the host of the television show *L'indice McSween* on Télé-Québec, and he also teaches administration at Cégep régional de Lanaudière à L'Assomption. He lives in Montreal.